God

is

God

God

is

God

Samson and other case histories
from the Book of Judges

by

John Hercus

HODDER AND STOUGHTON
LONDON SYDNEY AUCKLAND TORONTO

CONTENTS

ACKNOWLEDGMENT

Biblical quotations are from the New English Bible, Old Testament, © 1970 by permission of Oxford and Cambridge University Presses.

PROLOGUE

"In a sense we are lost, for we do drift about in rough and uncharted seas. We are fearful that if we do establish a steady course it may take us somewhere we do not want to go. We also know that the huge waves tossed up from the depths of conservative tradition and State authority may weaken, or even destroy us." So wrote Dale A. Johnson from his teaching desk at the University of California. And so would say teachers and students alike in many a centre if they were only willing and articulate enough to put their thoughts into words.

For the simple truth is that there are countless men in this sophisticated western world who share this sense of being utterly lost. Myriads, there are, who see life as being completely meaningless and pointless, a mere biological existence in which the naked ape that is *homo sapiens* is now the central figure of doom. Any sense that is beyond himself, says such a man, he cannot find and cannot even guess at. Lost—lost indeed! Fearful—yes, and why not?

So that there should be no surprise when so often we hear him declare that the obvious thing to do is just to grab what comes nearest to hand: the bellyful of rich food and good wine; the slick deal that will spin some coin into the till; the day lazing on the sun-drenched sands with the exciting challenge of the green surf pounding in on the beach; the sensuous thrill of the girl in his arms—these, he insists, are real. These are the things that make life become alive. These are what give purpose to his existence.

And then when the belly is empty; and when the cash has run out; and when the skies are black and the surf is flat; and, most of all, when the girl is in another's arms—why, then is the day of reckoning! Then the reality is no longer real; then even life is no longer alive; then these very things that he has counted on to bring purpose into existence turn out to be the things that drain the purpose out of existence. Then, indeed, he judges his life for what he has always feared it to be—a mere biological existence in which the naked ape that is *homo sapiens* is now the central figure of doom.

Full circle, he has gone, appetite to appetite, passion to passion, nothingness to nothingness, doom to doom. Meaningless, pointless, hopeless.

The suicide has his answer, of course, a complete answer. About a dozen people try this answer every single day in Sydney—about ten every week succeed. But the ape man sees full well that that answer is just the same as the question, and he's not quite as desperate as that. Not yet, at any rate.

The politician has his answer—the party intrigue and the tongue-in-cheek flattery of words. But that is just the cash deal again, and he's tried that.

The films, the huge world of mass-entertainment, has an answer, sure it has, and flashes it and flickers it and enlarges it and amplifies it and thunders it and cackles it on hi-fi and transistor alike. But as the lights come up and the sound goes off and the disc jockey stops for his prattling commercial the naked ape knows only too well what all that means— it's just the emptiness of the arms from which the girl has fled—and *that's* not an answer, *that's* a sword turned in a wound.

No wonder he's lost. No wonder he feels he's drifting on uncharted seas. How right he is, how deadly right, to fear any steady course, when everything in all this experience warns him that it might do it to him again. It might indeed be taking him somewhere he does not want to go.

No, the cruel, bitter experience is just the thing he feared: life is a mere biological existence in which the naked ape that is *homo sapiens* is now the central figure of doom.

Full circle indeed, doom to doom.

His father was not in this predicament. His father was

strengthened by cultural roots buried deep in the heart of Great Britain, he had supporting and stabilising factors that gave him ever so much more help. His father grew up in a community that was very constant, it was pretty much the same village, the same suburb, that it was in grandpa's time and great-grandpa's also. There was always the doctor in the dark brick house down on the main road corner; and even if the doctor didn't have any decent modern medical science to guide him, the doctor would always come to help at any time he was needed, and he would talk and advise and comfort. And the manager lived in the big stone house with the wide verandahs and the smooth lawns just outside the factory boundary. Dad lived very much the same sort of life that his dad had lived before him, and so it had gone on and on. Yes, and dad had had something else, something very much more sturdy even than the doctor and the manager and those other equally obvious, tangible social bulwarks. Dad had had the Church and the Crown and the Establishment. So that when the doctor died and when the manager retired, it was still no great problem: there was always God, King and Country. Why, dad had learned to say God, King and Country almost before he had learned to spell c-a-t cat; dad had always had God, King 'n' Country to hang on to, to have backing him up. And dad had the same God, King 'n' Country that his father had had before him and his father before that again. In fact God, King 'n' Country went back almost to the beginning of modern history and the only change was when it become God, Queen 'n' Country, and you could hardly say that made any real difference to dad.

But the naked ape has come a long, long way from those quaint, primitive, uncultured days. Those days when you just grew up and married and finally died in the place where you were born. Those days when there wasn't even a car in most homes and when flying was risky adventure and when radio was crackling experiment. Those days when vitamin and antibiotic and television weren't even words in the language. Those days when a man on the moon was still

Jules Verne science fiction.

No, today he is a mighty distance from those far-past times. Only half a century by the calendar clock, sure; but an endless age by the reckoning of life.

But the village life and the static community and that slow tempo and the horse-and-buggy transport are not the only things to have gone. God, King 'n' Country has gone, too. One world war made a wretched dent in the thin veneer on that flimsy structure. But a second world war has ripped the veneer clean off. And now the naked ape sees only too clearly the simple humanity of it all. That vast empire-building programme and that noble-hearted enthusiasm to educate the natives and make civilised citizens out of the heathen is not really a matter of God, King 'n' Country, it's just a matter of humans behaving like humans. For he sees, and sees to admire, those few bits of personal nobility and those many great big bits of courage and tenacity and adventure that got it all going—but that is just about the full measure of it. In fact, that's the trouble, for it *is* just about the full measure of it.

And nothing, nothing at all, so bewilders the ape man today as much as that. For he sees no God in it. No God in God, King 'n' Country. Human adventure, human courage, all the things that make *homo sapiens* the naked ape that in fact he is—but that is all he can find in it. No God. God is missing. And if there is in fact a god hidden away somewhere in the middle of it, then it's not the sort of god he's interested in. To bow down to that, to worship that, to dress up in best clothes and traipse off to cathedral or kirk or chapel and go through all that antiquated ritual just for that—no, he'd need to be more convinced about it than that. A whole lot more, indeed, if ever he's going to be persuaded to buy into low-rating stock like that.

So that it is in fact thus, it is in fact by much this method, that so many a man today has come to his position of isolation and disillusionment.

For he's been trained to think, to enquire, to probe and to analyse and to be critical. And it's the religion of his world, his own western world, that bewilders and disappoints him more than anything else he knows. It's Christendom, it's the great big cumbersome monolith of institutionalism and orthodoxy that is this white man's religion, that fills him with such utter dismay. For what he's seen of that, what he's heard from that, doesn't help one tiny bit. He started off by going to Sunday School—his dad used to send him off to Sunday School while dad himself read the Sunday comics before going off to golf; and when later in life he heard the taunt that God was just an Englishman twelve feet tall, he knew what was meant—it was the God of his Sunday School that was the butt of the taunt.

And when he was a kid his mother taught him to "say his prayers". Mum certainly didn't ever tell him what it was supposed to mean, and as he grew older she never taught him any new prayers. And he'd bet a million to one that his dad had long since forgotten every single prayer he'd ever learned. And he's heard the "prayers" that get flung about on Anzac Day and Armistice Day and Australia Day and lots of other Days, sure, he's heard plenty of "prayers". He's only glad he didn't go to one of those deadly "church" schools where they have chapel services thirteen times a week. Saturday night the fellows got a break from it. If the poor blighters hadn't built up a lifetime immunity after that sort of inoculation campaign they'd have finished up religious nuts or gone completely crackers!

And he's even heard records of "Land of Hope and Glory" —funny old 78s, but they weren't supposed to be funny, of course. But what a joke that was: "God who made thee mighty, make thee mightier yet", it went, and here we are, with not even an empire left. God didn't seem to be paying much attention to that "prayer", sure He didn't!

And he's god-father to a couple of nephews, and he just can't imagine what sort of crazy sense anybody can make out of that. For one of them lives in Canada and he hasn't even seen the kid yet, but Christendom says he can accept the responsibility for getting this unseen, across-the-world nephew into the kingdom of God. But what a laugh that really is, when he himself hasn't a clue in the world as to what the kingdom of God is supposed to be, he certainly hopes it turns out to be a better kingdom than the Land of Hope and Glory became.

And only yesterday he went to the funeral of his boss. There were over three hundred people present, most of them big shots in business; though he was only forty-one and was pretty fond of his grog and died of cirrhosis of the liver yet he was a mighty shrewd sort of business tycoon and wasn't really a bad sort of boss. But the way the padre "prayed" over the poor blighter you'd think he had already shaken hands with Saint Peter and was just on his way to a garden party with God Himself.

And, oh, there's so much like that, just think of Christmas, if ever there was one heck of a racket in the business world it's Christmas and the churches are packed full then and the sermons about it on the T.V. and on the radio are the most banal sentimental drivel you could dredge up from the bottom of any barrel and oh, what's the use, he's just had it ...

Yes, that's how it goes. That's just how it goes. For after nearly two thousand years of struggle and conflict, the human destinies of Christendom have fallen into the hands of this old, professional "Establishment". Think: this religion that started out because of the dynamic impact of a personal allegiance to a living God, now shrivelled away until it is just a statement of credo and acceptance by ethic. Just fancy: what was once the Empire-shattering momentum of a tiny group of mature men and women who faced life and who faced death because of their relationship of utter obedience to the will of God, now degenerated into a conglomerate institution where admission is by ritual and where approval is by conformity.

No wonder the naked ape is lost. No wonder he feels doomed. If that is the best guide his world can turn up, then no wonder he is so disturbed by the thoughts of the uncharted sea he is trying to cross.

Yet even that is not all. Even that is not the end. For there is another voice beginning to be heard, a voice that unsettles him more still. For this is a voice that is now telling him that it doesn't matter about God, it doesn't really matter if there even is a God, the thing that matters is man, so that what you need to know about God you can learn from the great spiritual qualities of man. "Why," says this voice, "it doesn't even matter what you do, any more than what you know—all you need to remember is to be filled with love. And for all practical purposes you can stop thinking about God altogether."

And the poor wretched modern man turns to see who it is that is making this statement, which bitter enemy of the Church, which hostile cynical foe from the outside world can this be—only to find to his utter bewilderment that it's not from the outside world at all! It's a new voice in Christendom itself! Not the atheist or the communist or the humanist or any other of those remarkable non-observers who can look at the ten thousand years of the greed and the war and the pride that make up recorded human history and who then say that mankind has his future securely within his grasp —no, it's not from one of them at all. No indeed. For it's a reactionary, abandon-the-sinking-ship group from the seminaries and theological halls of Christendom itself. It is this inner, eclectic band of the privileged that is making this remarkable statement. The age-old insistence of Christian experience that it is God Who is love, that love is indeed of God, that love must come from God to man if ever man is to have it at all—this, in devastating blatancy, is all being repudiated. Man is to be his own God. "Man has come of age"; is their remarkable finding: hence they derive their ultimate catchword, "God is dead".

No wonder the poor wretch is so hurt. Here he is, seeking and floundering and struggling to find meaning and direction and certainty and he's simply flattened. He's near to breaking-point. Often enough he's *at* breaking-point. For all too likely his home background and his personal experience have already dashed every hope and shattered every attempt at breaking out into a world of meaning and purpose and value. And now he's left reeling drunkenly under this ripping body blow which insists that his only security is what he can make for himself—and he's failed already. His real hope of goodness, he is being informed, lies in his capacity to love—and he's just filled with feelings of guilt and inadequacy and failure. If this is indeed the truth, he is at last realising, then his only hope is to escape into some fantasy experience, whether drug-induced or schizoid, where he can simply avoid the horrible reality. "Lost"; "drifting about"; "the huge waves ... may weaken or destroy us"— how truly spoken. For now, when he has turned to the Church, to the great institution of Christendom, pleading for bread, what cruel, heart-breaking stone is this that has been thrust into his hand?

Now if that were the end of the road then it would indeed be the end of the road. The end of all roads, in fact. The historians could put away their microphones and their stenographers could put the dust-covers over their electric typewriters and we could all stop taking any further notice of modern history. For only one word would need to be added to the total account of western culture, and that one word we would all be filling in for ourselves: *finis*.

But of course it's not the end. Not quite.

For there are still a few, perhaps a very few, who speak in another voice altogether. They may well be found within the walls of the vast institution that is Christendom, but not because they fit comfortably or easily there: they are there because it is the only common meeting-place they know.

And they may be speaking in its jargon and they may be heard repeating its dogmas and statements of credo—but that again is because this is very likely to be the only set of "spiritual" words they have learned. They may even be practising its rituals, less again because they have given them a clear philosophic and intellectual appraisal and approval, but rather because they have been simply human enough to accept what is generally accepted. But on one thing they are entirely united and different: they are convinced that they are here to serve God, and to serve God alone. That, for them, is the ultimate rule of life.

Yes, there are some like that. And, what is more, the ape man has almost certainly met some like that. He has even worked alongside some like that, in school, in university, in business. But they don't seem to understand him, and they speak in such a quaint jargon most of the time that he can't understand them; but there they are, and the naked ape knows full well that they have the sort of thing that he is seeking, they have the certainty and the purpose and the direction he so deeply feels he needs. Not that they are "better" people than he is, they are just about as commonplace and ordinary as everybody else is commonplace, they are just the same sort of naked ape that he is himself: but they have this other quality altogether. They are the people he most despises in life, for they seem to have abandoned their conflict with destiny; but they are still the people he most envies in life, for they have found their God.

Now it is from among these people, these people of certainty and conviction and confidence, that there is arising another group altogether. Again a group that is within the vast institutional boundaries of Christendom, but this time a thinking, questioning, attacking, avant-garde group of iconoclasts, people who utterly reject these two perversions of truth that have been masquerading as expressions of Christian faith, the one for centuries, the other for the last few decades only. They see only too clearly the selfishness of the juggernaut that would crush the penetrating mind of a Galileo or a Pascal just as it would crush the body of a More or a Cranmer; but equally they make no mistake as they measure the frailty of the human wisdom that is expressing its littleness through its pathetic attempt to see man as God because it can see God only as man. No, to both of these so-divergent attitudes they give an emphatic and intelligent denial, for they have all individually and responsibly entrusted their lives to the living Christ.

It should be no surprise to find that this group, this probing, enquiring, investigating group, includes many from a background of science. Men whose own personal experience of the reliability and trustworthiness of God as they have shared their lives with Him is now seen to be reflected in the reliability and trustworthiness of His laws in the universe they are exploring. Their world of science has always suffered its bitterest attacks from the citadel of organisational Christendom—hence, perhaps, their willingness to dispute the dicta and the inflexible stubbornness of the Establishment. Many of them are men of eminence, but that is not their strength—they draw their dynamic from their total allegiance to the Master they serve, the One Who literally broke the death-barrier. Of course they reject utterly and out of hand the authority of the Plato–Aristotle stream of Hellenism; whatever respect they may feel for the traditions of the past and however greatly they may admire the witness of the early fathers, such as Augustine, or of Aquinas, Luther or Calvin, they will pay them no true homage at all. For they will insist that their one all-binding loyalty is to Jesus Christ, and thus their only source of final authority must be the Bible.

They don't look in the Bible for proof of their science, any more than they expect their world of science to be bringing support to the Bible—what an absurdity that would be. The man who wants to brush up his mathematics would be naïve if he tried to do that by reading *Hamlet* or *A Midsummer Night's Dream*. And Piaggio and his *Differential Equations* is not going to do much to help the Shakespearian student either. Of course not! But these men will certainly insist that the few things they do learn about God from their research in science—His total concern for law and reliability and detail—are completely in character with the many, many things they learn about Him in the Bible. They realise that there are some simple people who seem to think of God as being rather pleased to be discovering all these exciting clues about astro-physics and D.N.A. synthesis and psycho-

analysis and even space travel. But they are not themselves
so deluded. God is not a fellow researcher, probing to find
the answers. God is the designer, He is the maker, He is
the utterly responsible and altogether trustworthy creator of
it all. Indeed, their own faith and witness may well be
summed up in the catchword: "God is *God*."

It is with a profound sense of gratitude to these men, and
it is also with an almost overwhelming feeling of humility
that this book is written—written in full awareness of a personal debt to so many of these eminent friends and teachers.
I can only trust that nobody will seriously think that I am
pretending to be acting as spokesman for them—the thought
is ridiculous. Just fancy, the poor man collecting crumbs
from under the table of the rich, even attempting to offer fare
to the guests of the table. Oh, no! The poor man doesn't
see himself for more than he is—the real source of wonderment must lie in understanding how rich are the crumbs.

For this book is the personal outcome of this lavish fare.
The exciting physical and biological insights into the origin
and nature of man; the psychological concepts and understanding of the mechanism of guilt and guilt-feeling; the
enormous wealth of scholarship in the realms of archaeology
and biblical studies—some of these are intended to be
expressed in these pages.

For altogether in the experience of these rich men (and
of this one poor one) is the controlling conviction that there
is complete meaning and purpose in life. Not because some
are rich, still less because this one is poor, but because in
absolute truth, God is *God*.

Now I'm only a doctor. I'm not a professional philosopher.
So that I don't plan to debate all this. Not that I think it
can't be debated or shouldn't be debated. But that is not my
task here. People are my business, usually people in trouble
or need, and it is from this privileged vantage-point of an
ordinarily successful medical practice, with its unique free-

dom of penetration into the very heart and being of people, that I am writing.

For this book is all about people. If there is any philosophy (and there will be some) it is quite incidental; and if there is any doctrine (and there will be quite a bit) then it will be deliberately unobtrusive. But it will be altogether about the day-to-day and life-to-death experiences of people.

For people are in fact my business ...

But which people? It would certainly seem easy enough, and perhaps rewarding enough, to take you into my own case histories, to introduce you to a few selected records of the vast number of people I have met in my ordinary medical life. In this highly privileged encounter of doctor and patient there is a certain unique access to the most hidden recesses of hope and fear, success and failure, joy and despair. And repeat this about five thousand times a year, and repeat *that* each year for over a quarter of a century, and any doctor who has been a doctor and not just a medical technician will have a whole life full (and a heart full) of the things that would fill any book in the world. I could certainly do that, and with just the tiny bit of skill and imagination that would be necessary to change the names and the personal data enough to preserve true anonymity, then another Cronin (or even Kildare) could arise.

But I don't want to do that. For I will be asking questions that medical science won't answer, won't even pretend to answer. Medicine is concerned with machinery: intra-cellular enzyme mechanisms, anti-cholinergic blocking agents, techniques in surgical procedures, how many days off work—things like that. It is built on precise knowledge of anatomy, exact estimates of function, predictable changes in pathological processes—more things like that. Just which cog is it that is broken, which bearing is running hot, how can this fuel line be cleared—you may almost think of it as biological engineering, very often. And even the highly complex wonder of emotional response—the "psycho-somatic" story, the "mind-over-matter" of thirty years ago —even that is now falling into the same category, as the laws of the activity and of the predictability of human behaviour are at last grouping themselves alongside the laws of pathology and of pharmacology. *That* is medicine. That is the field of responsibility of a modern medical school.

No, not my case histories. Nor any other doctor's case history notes, either.

For in any case, the lost, drifting, fearful man of this modern age isn't finally interested in these questions. He gets answers to them from every digest and journal and magazine and T.V. network in the land. He's being bombarded with so much medical science, psychiatric case-work and space physiology that he hardly knows which is fact and which is fiction. And he's seen a hole in the heart repaired on the small screen on the T.V.; and he's just seen a baby being born on the big screen in the cinema; and altogether he hopes that his luck will hold out enough to save him from needing to be dragged to pieces by this same relentless search and probe of surgical technology—no, thank you! Those aren't the things that bother him.

It's the reason. And the purpose. And the objective. Not what is it that's happening—but why is it that it's happening? Not a question of the machinery inside, but a question of the machinery outside.

So that you see, perhaps, why my case history notes won't do. Why they won't do enough. For I'm only another naked ape, too. I'm just another sample specimen of *homo sapiens* like any other modern man. And I'm asking the same questions.

But I'm one of the few, fortunate ones who have found some of the answers. I haven't found them in science or medicine, any more than I have found them in philosophy or current affairs. (And I confess I haven't bothered to ask in politics.)

No, I have found the answers in God. To be more accurate, I should say that I have found the answers from God. I have met God. I keep meeting God. To be more accurate still, I should say that God has met me and that God keeps meeting me. And it is from Him, and from Him alone, of course, that any of these answers can come.

But just telling you my experience is not going to help you. It is very hard to learn from anybody else's experience. That is not my idea at all. Not my medical case history notes, certainly; and not my personal autobiographical experiences, even more certainly.

What I am in fact setting out to do is to take you into some case records God has Himself preserved concerning some people, to tell us His side of their story. His accounts of how He met some of them, spoke to them, crossed purposes with them. And the records I will be studying with you are of people whose personal experiences make our bitter, disturbed naked ape of today seem almost tame and tranquil by comparison. So that if God can show us from their lives and happenings how some sense is to be discovered; if He can make meaning out of their lives, then we may well be able to look again at our modern world and expect to see a bit more clearly what is really going on here.

Remember, it is the people in it, the struggling, near-to-breaking-point wretches involved in all this, that we will be watching. We will have eyes and ears (and heart) only for the people caught up within it. For it is the people God is telling us about. It is to them that God is directing us.

Now I'm going to allow myself one single yardstick of measurement—the yardstick of God's judgment. If God tells me that He is Himself responsible for something that happens, and it seems impossible to me I didn't ever imagine God could be like that, hadn't we better stop and debate all this like the old Greek philosophers and divide life into Good and Evil with what we like as Good and what we don't like as Evil—then no. No dice! I'll just stop and listen to God Himself, and if I can't understand it, then I'll be wise to ask God to make me humbler and less opinionated and more willing to let Him tell me what He is like. And again: if He says a man is a failure, then that man is a failure no matter what I might have thought about him. And if everything about a fellow had seemed to me to be dreadful and hopeless and altogether thumbs-down, and God says he's

OK, then he's OK and that's all there is to it. I'm not going
to tell God what goes, remember I'm trying to find out what
God thinks, not what John Hercus or any other mere man
thinks. I can hear men's opinions any old day of the week,
plenty of them. But God's opinion is the one that matters.
God is God, remember, and though He says we are made
in His image, that doesn't for a moment imply that He is
made in ours. We are creatures, we are made of matter—
"dust" is the rather unflattering word God Himself uses
about us. He is not saying that to belittle us or to slap us
down or to tell us what useless so-and-so's we are. Nonsense! That was one of the mistaken ideas the Greek philosophers had about life. But I'm not studying God's word
just to find that man-made thinking. No, thank you! Let
us keep to the facts as God tells them, and let us remember
that we are just men. But let us also be very careful to
remember that it is in the life of a normal man, *homo sapiens*
is the biological jargon term, that God is moving and working, to make something altogether different out of him. And
that is what the Bible is really all about, for God says that
is what life is all about.

So I am taking you to some stories God has preserved.
Stories of human courage and human skill just as much as
they are stories of human bitterness and human hatred. Some
"they all lived happily ever afterwards" stories; and some
heart-breaking tragedies: but all of them God's stories. And
all of them about people just like ourselves.

But there is something special about these people—for
four of the men we will be reading about have their names
in the most celebrated Honours Roll ever compiled. God's
Honours Roll. In the New Testament, one of the writers
gives a list of some of the celebrated "men of faith". There
are sixteen names in that ultra-select short list, fourteen
men and two women. And no less than four of these fourteen men are among those we will be studying. Barak,
Gideon, Jephthah and Samson, those four men are, and God
has got those four men among those listed Great Ones.

And please let me make this quite clear: if God says

those men are "in", if He says they have made the top grade,
if He approves them—then that is exactly all there is to say.
They are "in", they are top grade, they are most certainly
approved. Listen: when I read of a man that "he had pleased
God"; of another that "he made good his claim to righteous-
ness"; of another that he was "as one who saw the invisible
God"; of all of them that "God is not ashamed to be called
their God"; that God says "they were too good for this
world"—when I read that sort of thing, then I go on record
as insisting that those are the really top men of history.
Forget their university degrees, a fig for their political
achievements, just wipe all their bank balances. All that
human bric-à-brac is mere trash when compared with God's
riches, when measured against the measurements of Heaven.

And when I remember that these were only men, all of
them, the ordinary everyday common or garden variety like
the rest of us, yet they all finished up by having God say
that sort of thing about them, why, then, everything inside
me is stirred as I have never experienced before. That, before
all else, is the thing I long for most. To discover that, to be
given that—to have that transcending acceptance by God—
please, dear God, I am asking, please let me in on that. For
then, indeed, life assumes reality; then, assuredly, the past
becomes purpose and the future finds real goal as the
present fills with meaning. Then, at last, we may say that
man becomes Man.

So that it is to the Book of Judges, the seventh book in
the Bible, that I am now taking you, to learn from God
what He says life is all about. Not in philosophy, not in
politics, not even in religion: but in the conflict and turmoil
of life and death itself. Then, and then alone, may we understand how truly God is *God*.

EHUD, THE LEFT-HANDED BENJAMITE

The people were in trouble. Real trouble. Desperate, right-up-to-the-neck trouble.

They were hungry. They lived in hovels, often still in tents made of animal skins and goats' hair. They had practically no tools or arms or metals. They had no cash. They were dead flat broke. And what is more, they lived on the hilltops and rocky fastnesses and barren slopes of the harsh, inhospitable mountain country, eking out a precarious hand-to-mouth existence with little comfort, less pleasure and no relaxation at all.

It was pitiful. It was relentless. It was hopeless.

And it was not going on just for a few months. Not even for a few years. It wasn't simply for a few decades. It seemed to be going on for centuries ...

Yet none of this gives the proper picture clearly. Our ancient British ancestors didn't fare much better, all those long centuries of cave life and woad-painting before Julius Caesar. The Australian aboriginal survived thousands and thousands of years under the relentless challenge of a vast land that contained no single animal capable of domestication and not one plant capable of being developed for crop or harvest. The Eskimo has survived to this very day in a world of perpetual, unyielding ice, where even wood is non-existent except as driftwood.

No. The people were in trouble, but the real poignancy did not merely lie in bleak countryside and inhospitable terrain. Not a bit. The real hurt, the iron that ate into their souls, lay in the fact that down in the valleys just below them, there on the plains and river flats that lay spread out almost at their very feet—down there it was lush, fertile, rich.

Yes, it was this bountiful wealth of the low country that so taunted them and jeered at them for their poverty and hunger. For the people in the valleys were long-established, well fortified, richly cultured. Big, clever, strong people who sneered at them in their penury and wretchedness. No hope in the world of ever being able to dash down the hillside and oust these long-entrenched nations. To start a war like that you need weapons and trained fighters and good supply lines. And all they had was sticks and stones, spears and arrows, clubs and bare fists—no arms, no metal even to make arms out of. And no free time to spend like that at the smithy or at the forge, even if they had had the metal.

Pitiful. Relentless. Hopeless.

And year after year, decade after decade.

So that I can't blame them, and I'm sure you won't either, for doing what they did. They did what all sensible, prudent, practical men of affairs and of business had done before that and are still doing today: if you can't beat them, join them. They had no hope of conquering the valleys, but they could go and sell themselves into slavery with the people down in the plains.

In fact they did then, and that was over three thousand years ago, what hundreds of millions of Eastern people are doing at this very time: rushing headlong into the lavish richness of the valley of western materialism in their clamour for the extravagance of our cultural tinsel.

No, I don't blame them. But God did. He was furious. This, He insisted, was the dead end. This was beyond the pale. This He would never tolerate or forgive.

Because these were the very people He had dragged *out* of slavery. This was the race He had snatched right from under the very nose of the great Pharoah, king of Egypt. Yes, God kept insisting, He had rescued them from Pharoah Rameses, had provided them with food and water in the arid, parched hopelessness of the Sinai desert for a whole generation. And here they were, finally in a land of their

own, free at last of all the shackles of slavery, now deliberately tossing it all away and going back into bondage. And
all just for the sake of a bigger bellyfull of food and prettier
rags to wear on their backs!

God was really annoyed. And He said so. And God did
what He always does—He backed up what He said by what
He did.

And that is what this tale is about ...

When first they came into Palestine, the Israelites had
been able to batter their way into the land and get a few
good footholds in the hills. But that was really just about
all. Now and again they mopped up a tiny fortified town
or two, and captured a little bit of grazing land—but no
more. None of this "Invasion of Britain" stuff by Julius C.,
with his Roman roads and Roman towns and Roman bridges
and Roman garrisons. Sure, Caesar specialised in that sort
of thing, and here we are, all these centuries later, with some
of our kids still learning Latin verbs at school. But it was
not like that with the Israelites. No. Nothing in the very
least bit like that. For when they came into Palestine they
carried in their hands and on their backs every single possession they had in all their world. No writing back to Egypt
for mum to send out a Christmas hamper and a few knitted
woollies. No signalling back to G.H.Q. for another infantry
division and replacements for the armoured vehicles. They
had escaped out of slavery, remember, and forty years mill-
ing round in the desert hadn't given them any better equipment or made them any wealthier.

So that as year succeeded year and generation finally
succeeded generation, the whole climate of opinion began
to change. Any clear, strong allegiance to God began to
yield to arguments of hunger and isolation, and first one,
then another, would give up. Always down into slavery.
Anything rather than the bitter, tough, hand-to-mouth
struggle that the isolated hilltop life demanded.

It was an open, head-on clash—God saying one thing,
the people saying and doing the exact opposite.

Let us watch, as we see how God handles such an impasse. Let us learn, as we try to understand His answer to such a deadlock. And then perhaps we may expect some little insight into the ordinary day-to-day experiences in our own lives: for the God who lived in those centuries-gone times is just the same today ...

The tribe of Benjamin had got itself established on some of the hill country just to the west of the Jordan, and there they were hanging on in grim and precarious peril. Weak, tiny, scattered, even their tribal unity was a token more than a reality. No established leadership, no central government, no public service, no focalised social organisation at all. And there on the plains just below them was Jericho, the City of Palms. Not really much of a place, and to our sophisticated western eyes a very tin-pot little mud village indeed. But to the ragged, hungry, struggling Israelites it was Regent Street, Fifth Avenue and the Champs Elysées all in one. No magnet ever attracted needles and nails and knives as Jericho attracted them. Down to Jericho, with its wealth and its strength and its security, they began to drift.

Now over to the south-east, and just across the Jordan— Dead Sea Valley, was the little country of Moab. The Moabites were a sort of close national cousin to the Israelites. They were descended from Lot, Abraham's nephew. But they had settled in their tiny tableland just between the Jordan valley and the Arabian desert, settled now for over a hundred years, and were very strongly dug in.

The chieftain of Moab at the time was a great big blubbery mountain of a man who delighted in the name of Eglon. Eglon wasn't just large—he was enormous. He wasn't a bit overweight—he was disgustingly obese. He wasn't like the twenty-stone wrestler on the T.V.—he was like the thirty-six stone fat man in the side-show. Something like four hundredweight. Two hundred kilos.

But if you are thinking of Eglon as one of those big, happy, generous-hearted Mr. Pickwicks of life, then you are just so wrong. Eglon was not that sort of man at all. For

fat and all that he was as a clinical specimen, there was
nothing soft about Eglon as a ruler. Nothing the least little
bit soft. And he had teamed up with some Amalekites from
his south and some Ammonites from his north, and across
the Jordan they had streamed. It wasn't any longer a matter
of the Benjamites packing up and going off to Moab—it
was a case of Moab arming up and going off to Benjamin.

And the impact of this power-pact alliance began to
squeeze the last drop of life-blood out of the Hebrew settlers
in the hill country within their pincer-grip. As these desperately stricken people squirmed and struggled in his iron-
hard military gauntlet, Eglon himself sat back and collected
the boodle.

There he lolled, the whole four hundredweight of him,
in the cool-shaded bower he had built on the rooftop of
his house, the fanning of his flunkeys helping lessen the
overloading of his heat-regulating mechanism that such a
grossly disturbed surface-mass ratio had saddled him with.
It takes little imagination to see him still, squatting in gross
obesity on his outsize throne, as the crippling and ruinous
levy that was laid on his subject people was brought to him
and spread at his feet.

This is Eglon, king of Moab. About 1200 B.C. Big flabby
Eglon. But nothing soft. Nothing soft at all. Not in Eglon.

And certainly no fool, either. He knew how to look after
himself, and you can say that again. For any big mountain
of a man who spends his day sitting out in the sub-tropical
heat and sun under the Middle East sky is still going to be
hot and sticky with sweat, and his mouth is going to be as
dry as parchment. My, he will be thirsty!

But Eglon is one of those kings who believes in himself
and in his own comfort, and he knew what to do about it.
Long, cool drinks, and plenty of them, why, that's the
obvious answer. What's the use of being king if you can't
even get comfortable?

"Yes," I hear you say, "good for you, Eglon, you know
how to go about it. But listen, Eglon, you don't need to be
a twentieth-century medico to know enough simple renal

physiology to guess what is going to happen. As you lean
back in that huge cushioned throne of yours, following one
cooling mug of beer with another the same, please, you
are heading for trouble. Just nuisance trouble, I know, but
trouble all the same. For you will very soon find that you
will need to heft that great hulking body of yours out of
its so-relaxing seat, and off you will need to go. Clamber
down the stairs, out across your little backyard, and get
comfortable. Then back in the blazing sun, lumbering up
those stairs again, and bless your soul, Eglon, once more
you will be puffing and blowing and hot and sweating like
nothing on earth, and the whole thing will have gone full
circle. Your mouth will be getting dry even before you get
back to the top of the stairs, and so it's more to drink and
more overloading of excretory physiology—and off you
traipse again. Eglon, isn't that rooftop bower a bit of a
mistake? Wouldn't it have been better to have set yourself
up in the garden, perhaps, just a short walk under a shady
level covered way to reach your You-Know-What, and
altogether a lot better in the end?"

If you think like that, then you have misunderstood your
Eglon. Underestimated him badly. For Eglon sat there, great
rolls of fat hanging from jowl and paunch alike, and was
as comfortable as you could wish. For he had got in three
thousand years ahead of the modern architect and home-
building expert. He had got himself a nice, convenient,
upstairs, rooftop toilet. None of this puffing and blowing
and panting as he had to clamber up and down those stairs
—not for Eglon. A heave, and his two hundred or so kilos
was on its feet, a few short steps and he could slam the door
and he was right. No embarrassment, no prying eyes to see
how disgustingly undignified a great blubbery human form
like this can really be—nothing like this for Eglon, thank
you ...

And you sit there and wonder just what all this is about.
Shouldn't God be concerned with "spiritual" things? All
this reference to sanitation is vulgar even beyond the T.V.

shows and Hollywood. You must know this. Isn't religion supposed to lift men's eyes to purer, nobler heights? Should not thoughts of God make a man forget the merely natural, earthly, bodily world altogether and lead him to reflect on the sublime and the ultimate and the beyond? And such an utter vulgarity as urinal facilities for relief of disturbed fluid balance is embarrassing even to talk about.

Then let me say, as kindly as I may but as firmly as I must, that if you think like that then you have never really tried to find out what God Himself says He is like. Remember, it was the God who designed the Milky Way who also designed the nephron and the collecting tubule. Yes, it was the mind that conceived the sunset and the rainbow and the rose in full bloom that also allowed the tornado and the tubercle bacillus and the malignant cell. For there is no truth more consistently and insistently stated in the Bible than this. The whole philosophy of the Christian faith hinges on this limitless claim: it is because of his part in creation that Christ is himself worthy of our worship. "No single thing was created without him"; "he created all orders of existence"; "in him everything in heaven and on earth was created, not only things visible but also the invisible"; "the whole universe has been created through him and for him". And if this puzzles you, if this is not what you had naturally supposed God is like and that you'd never have thought that all the wretchedness of human experience could ever be associated with God, then Saint Paul says that he, too, is "groaning inwardly" under it—but this is the very basis for his pungent statement: "the created universe was made the victim of frustration, not by its own choice, but because of him who made it so".

Indeed, it's because we do find this hard to understand, it is because we would find it much simpler if God had been made like us instead of being God—it is because of all this that God has seen fit to tell us the truth about Himself. There is one God, and one only. And neither heaven nor hell, far less this little earth itself, will ever contain any other.

Now I said that I didn't want to debate these matters, however worthy of debate they may well be, but I do want to see how this great truth works out in life—so on with the story. For it was just this sort of problem that stopped me getting along with it. It was this very obesity of fatty Eglon, his insistent and awkward physiological urges, and his embarrassed need for privacy in attending to those urges, that God used to end it all! These same things, that rather revolt our aesthetic sophistication, are shown by God to be the actual machinery that He will employ to free the tyranny binding His people. God is most certainly *not* made in man's image.

You can guess as easily as kiss your hand what it was like in Benjamin, now. For the Moabite thrust had penetrated right into Benjamin and Judah, right across the almost impassible Jordan. Indeed, Jericho, which had been the very first town they had ever captured after entering Palestine— Jericho, the City of Palms—belonged to Eglon. Eglon owned Jericho! And even if he didn't live there, even if he had his rooftop arbour with the personal privacy and convenience of that toilet in his own Moabite capital, Jericho belonged to him. There were Eglon's men, right in their own country, right there in the city of Jericho.

God had stopped it, and that's for sure. Stopped it dead. This casual drift of His people into Moab was finished. Washed right up. All the Benjamite lads with their thoughts of the pretty Moabite girls, all the Benjamite lasses with their dreams of the wolf-whistles from the attractive Moabite beaux in Main Street—all this was now a thing of the past. Eglon had fixed all that. Any Israelite youth who now came rolling down the hill road, knapsack slung over his shoulder, on his way to Moab and success—why, that kid was just plain mad. The chains were round that fellow before he could even brush the sweat from his eyes and see who it was that had caught him! For Eglon was king. Fat, greedy, piggy-eyed Eglon. And Eglon had ended all that.

What a pitiful plight the people were in. Their precarious existence on the mountains was bad enough, surely, but now

they were under the economic thumb of the big greedy
monster, Eglon, and he was crushing them to their final
death. No escape. No possible way out. They were done.

And the people of Benjamin did what men *in extremis*
have often done—they cried to God in their despair. And
God heard them.

God always hears men when they really mean what they
are praying. God is not in the least bit embarrassed by this
despairing, desperate cry in man. In fact it's a question
whether God hears any other sort of cry at all. It's the man
beating on his breast in utter despair, with his "O God, have
mercy on me" whose voice really reaches Heaven. It's the
well set-up and utterly satisfied pundit who is so full of
congratulation for his vast moral and religious advantages,
his "I thank Thee, O God, that I am not like the rest of
men", who is not heard. His "prayer" of self-approval stays
entirely within his own little corner of the temple and doesn't
even reach the ceiling rafters. Like the "God, get me out of
this slit trench" of World War II, the "God, help the doctor
to get all the roots out" of the cancer patient, the "God, I
simply must pass this exam. You'd better help me" of the
student.

But the Benjamites weren't just chatting to God. They
weren't just complaining to God. They were desperate. They
meant it.

"When they cried to the Lord for help, he raised up a
man to deliver them, Ehud son of Gera the Benjamite, who
was left-handed."

You see what I mean? Even the right and the left-
handedness of life is important to God. And Ehud was left-
handed.

Now Ehud was actually planning a trip to Moab. He was
going on a visit to Eglon. He wasn't going there to try and
escape from the wretched misery of his people up on the
hilltop. No, not a bit like that. He was going to Moab to
take the tribute to Eglon. He was the official spokesman, he
was the tribal representative. He and his party had to cart
away all that hard-to-spare tax and pay it over into the big,

fat, greedy hand of Eglon. Remember, cash on demand. No credit. No promissory notes. Not with Eglon. He liked the payment brought right into his cool, comfortable roof-chamber, and no monkeying about with fiduciary note issues and share exchanges. No credit cards. No Diner's Club tick. Nothing like that for big-bellied Eglon. No, sir! Cash on the button.

And the cash was in kind. Just how those starving, impoverished people of Benjamin could pay over anything except I.O.U.s it is hard to guess, but they did. Meat, perhaps. Or hides and fleeces. Woven goods, or plaited—all those things that the women made, things so valuable in the rugged economy of the hill dwellers' lot—now handed over to Eglon.

And Ehud, left-handed Ehud, led the party that took the tribute.

I don't know how many such trips Ehud had made. His father Gera was probably the tribal chieftain and this landed the job in his family lap; but just how many such miserable journeys had fallen to the lot of this household I can't even guess. I rather think that Ehud had done it several times at least, but whether none or many he decided that this was going to be his last. For he had an extra item with him, an addition to the levied bounty he was due to hand over to Eglon. Not part of the tribal tribute, not something Eglon was expecting. Just his own personal, parting gift to Eglon. It was a sword!

Now nothing jewel-encrusted, no fine swordmaker's craftsmanship about this sword. No, it was for utility, not for ornament. Yet nothing common, none of this mass-produced modern junk. Not this one. It was a special, a "one-off" item. It was for Eglon!

Just a little sword. About fifteen inches long, that's all. Just a bit of a dagger, really. But a king-sized dagger! An Eglon-sized dagger! Long enough to knock a considerable hole in a man, yet short enough to strap on to his thigh and never betray its menacing presence by a single glancing flash from its two sharp-honed edges or by the tiniest hint of a limp or halt in his gait.

A lovely little sword! Eglon's sword!

What a scene. What a tale. Can't you picture it in every imagination-teasing detail? Great big fat Eglon with his sharp beady little eyes, deep-set in their cold, unblinking stare in all that mountain of blubbery fat. Missing nothing, as they swivel to and fro in their sockets, their quick darting movements avoiding the ponderous, energy-consuming, heat-producing turning of head and neck.

But sharp and penetrating as his flashing eye-movements might be, there is no hustling and bustling about the scene. As Ehud comes into the roof-chamber, his carriers following with their precious tribute load, Eglon is not the one to hurry it along. Plenty of time; these big fat slobs just hate anything that smacks of haste, movement and sweat. Time for a proper ceremonial, something that will really impress these cringing Yids. Something that will keep them in their place, make them eat humble pie, show them who's boss. But no risks either. Careful, impressive ceremonial, but certainly no risks. Make sure the right arm is bare—no weapon tucked into a sleeve. Make them bow, make them kneel on the left knee as the right arm is raised in token of deference. Very awkward for a man to spring to his feet from that off-balance position. No risks.

Sure, I'm guessing when I say that it took place like that, but I'm also sure I'm guessing pretty close to the mark. Why, you may know, as I know, of ceremonial that even today is patterned along just this same form. But whatever the precise pattern, the result is what we are interested in—the sudden flash of steel as that little dagger is whipped from his right thigh, and Ehud has given Eglon the last bit of Benjamite tribute he will ever receive.

And we peer excitedly, eyes staring eagerly, to watch it happen. For Ehud is left-handed, his bare right arm, raised in deferential salute, doesn't mean a thing, the kneeling on his left knee gives Eglon no protection at all. We watch, and we watch ...

There is a lot of shuffling and movement as the bearers

come filing past, depositing their hard-earned loads in front of the king, his tally clerks marking each item off against their levy lists. And we can scarcely even dare to allow ourselves the luxury of blinking, so intent are we to keep close watch on Ehud, waiting for the quick split-second lunge as the deadly little sliver of metal will flash into action. There he is, kneeling with head bowed at the very feet of the king, no tell-tale sign of the murderous weapon with its double razor-sharp edge. And we watch. And we watch ... And we watch ...

And it's over. The tribute is all checked and counter-checked, the receipts are all made out, the visit is at an end. Ehud rises, they bow deferentially, they back their respectful way out of the presence—they are gone! The dagger is still bright and clean, not a single drop of Moabite blood even on its very tip. Ehud has failed!

Perhaps you see even more clearly still just what I mean about God. This completely calm, undisturbed way of simply reporting the affairs of men in this apparently cold, indifferent, laconic fashion. Is this merely God's way of reminding us that He is unimpressed, that He is scarcely interested, that He is "Out There"? Nonsense! What preposterous drivel. As God sees so clearly what we see only in imagination, as He watches Ehud come, and then go, why, He is concerned, so deeply concerned, that He has already planned, ages beyond ages ago, to come here and die as man Himself—that is what God is really like. This is not casual indifference, this is the sign of His complete understanding, His deep sympathy and insight and concern that arises from knowing every single detail of the thought-configurations in the whole of a human personality.

They are miles and miles down the road home. Long, sad and dusty miles. They have reached Gilgal. Right across the Jordan, there they are, stopping for a short rest in the shadow of the Sculptured Stones, a rather famous little local tourist attraction. The men are miserable, as men must always be miserable when they have just had to hand over all those precious extras, those personal valuables that make so very much difference in the comfort of home. That sour taste in the mouth of any tax-payer today who has just paid his income-tax is almost honey-sweet compared to the ashen bitterness in the experience of these wretched Benjamites resting under the shade of the Sculptured Stones at Gilgal.

But what about Ehud? Think how he must have felt. As he stepped round to the other side of the Stones and quickly slipped the dagger from his right thigh, think of the turmoil in his mind. For he had been sure he was supposed to kill Eglon, he had been certain he was right in planning that. All the leading-up factors had pointed so clearly that way. When he first knew he was chosen to lead the tribute-paying party; when he first realised the significance of his luck in finding that precious piece of bronze to make into a dagger; being so further in luck in gaining the time and energy to shape and hone it—he knew he had heard the voice of God correctly. God had been asking him to kill Eglon. Ehud was sure he had got it straight. But more still, being lucky enough to be left-handed, kneeling in that awkward position on his left knee with his right hand upraised —why, he was obviously right in planning it this way.

And yet he had simply not had a chance. It wasn't just a matter of being scared of starting a brawl and perhaps getting killed—that was a risk he was quite prepared for. It was the risk of failing. The risk of making a wild lunge at the big tubby king and just grazing him. Perhaps just slicing into the outer six or eight inches of blubber and not reaching his vitals. That was the problem. For he had practised and practised for hour after long hour, he had been over and over it all in his mind until every minute detail was sharp-etched into his inmost being—and it had just not worked out right. The distance was a few inches too great, Eglon was sitting too far back in his big chair, there had been too many Moabites right alongside the king, there had been too many eyes watching him closely and personally —no, he simply couldn't do it.

My, how miserable Ehud felt! He felt just rotten. God had set the whole job up for him, and given him the absolute chance of a lifetime to make something really good out of his life—and he had flopped. He picked up the little sword again, felt its fine light balance again, ran his finger-tips down those two razor-sharp edges again—that dagger that was still not used.

But there was nothing wrong with the dagger itself. No, that was not the trouble. It was he himself. He was the trouble. He had simply missed his chance. Had dipped out.

Or had he? Was this perhaps the way God wanted it? Was this really God's way of doing it? Let me think, now ...

There was just that slight tightening of the eyelids and brows, just a hint of firmness in the setting of his jaw, just a tiny spring in his step, that could have conveyed a message, if only his glum followers had been alert enough to sense it.

For Ehud was back again among his fellows, as they picked up their now so-light packs, to set off up the road for home again. And perhaps just the ring in his voice, just those few, nearly inconspicuous details, to tell us that Ehud is somehow different.

"Look, chaps. I'm going to leave you. I have an idea. I'd like to try it out. I can't tell you what it is, but you go on. I want to try something. If I don't catch up with you by tomorrow night then I probably won't ever be back at all. But if I'm lucky I'll be with you before you get far into the hills. So long, good luck."

And with a lightness of step that matched the firmness of his voice, Ehud turned on his heel and strode back along the Moab road.

"Hey, fellers, look who's coming! It's Ehud, blest if it isn't."

"Well, what do you know? Only just paid over his tribute dues this morning, and back again so soon. What on earth can he be after?"

"Perhaps he's come back to pay over some more. Perhaps he just likes paying tribute to Eglon."

"Ha! Mesha, that's not bad! Not bad at all! That's

nearly as funny as hoping to get a refund."

And the burst of laughter from Eglon's attendants started a whole spate of ribaldry and cross-chat as they peered over the balustrade round the guard-room, watching Ehud come striding up the Gilgal road.

"Heck! Fancy anybody wanting to come back here! Just deliberately coming back to Eglon!"

"You're just so right. We're terrified of him ourselves, and we don't mind saying so, and we work for him. We're the people he trusts. But fancy a lousy Benjamite actually wanting to come back!"

"Perhaps he's mad."

"Yeah! Perhaps he needs to see an analyst. Perhaps the psychiatrists in his own territory are too mad to help him."

"OK. Come on, men. On your feet." This from the N.C.O. in charge. "Let's go and meet him and find out what does actually bring him back."

Ehud was striding up the road, each pace an inch longer in length and a moment shorter in time than a mere traveller, a tourist, a casual visitor, would take. The Moabite guards couldn't miss the obvious urgency that his gait was expressing. But as he came near, as a couple of mouths opened to hail him in ribald contempt, his pursed lips, his eyebrows raised over staring eyes, his hand held out in restraining gesture, all silenced them instantly, without the "Shhh." that even at that distance they could hear from his lips.

His step did not falter, its pace did not slacken a fraction, as he stepped right into their circle, stopping abruptly with his face only half a yard from the sergeant in charge.

"Gentlemen. Something terribly important. I'll have to tell Eglon. Quick!" The hoarse whisper carried an air of utterly compelling urgency. In a moment they were in action.

"Sir." The Moabite attendants who moved cautiously into Eglon's presence could hardly suppress their concern and excitement.

"Sir, it's Ehud. The Israelite envoy. The Benjamite. He's back. He's waiting. Says he must see you. He says he has a very important message for you and he won't tell us what it is."

"Yes, sir. He's paid all his taxes, you remember. Quite a good lot of stuff, and we had no trouble with him at all. He says it's got nothing to do with that. He says it's terribly urgent."

"Sir, it really looks as though he must have come across something, he's all dusty and covered in sweat, he must have been running like mad to try and get here."

"I think it must be something to do with the gods, sir. I asked him that, and his eyes just flashed at me and he said, 'I've a message for Eglon, your great king. Just take me to him.' If he hadn't been so serious I'd have laid his jaw open for being so insolent. I really think you should see him, sir."

Eglon's beady, malevolent eyes just bored into the faces of his attendants as they burst out with their tale. But his voice was nearly reduced to a whisper, was almost a mere purring, as he answered, "Bring Ehud in. This interests me. I shall be delighted to meet Ehud again so soon. I am always glad of the gifts my Benjamite subjects can bring, whether they be in taxes or even in information. Let me hear what he has to say."

His voice was soft, almost effeminate; but the slight hint of a smile belonged only to his teeth, there was no trace of it in his eyes, no suggestion of friendly gesture, no possibility of gentleness. Not with Eglon.

But his servants knew their chief, and they moved to obey. Slowly, no hurry, of course, in Eglon's presence. All nice and smooth and steady, they rose and withdrew, to return in a few moments with Ehud. Ehud and his little sword!

As the Benjamite came in and sank on to his left knee, his bared right arm raised again in the salute that only that morning had been made in this exact same spot, everybody in the room could see the excitement that gripped him. The slightly staring eyeballs with their wide-open pupils, the beads of perspiration that the temperature of the room could not alone explain, the faint tremble in the outstretched arm, most of all the hoarseness in his voice as he began to speak through too-dry lips: "Sir! A fantastic bit of luck! I found it out by the sheerest fluke. You'd hardly believe it could happen, but it did, and I dashed back to tell you."

It was superbly done. It was inspired. It was worthy of a Garrick. Olivier would have been proud of it. It captured the whole house. An excited ripple of sound broke out from the attendants. But only for a moment. A short, sibilant "Silence!" from Eglon, and the murmur died even faster than it had begun. Eglon sat quite still, a great mountain of utterly motionless flesh, even his breathing, which usually demonstrated some of the respiratory embarrassment occasioned by his obesity, was now slow and shallow. The very stillness of his gaze compelled Ehud to continue.

"But, sir ..." And Ehud stopped, raised his head to look straight into the king's eyes, his upraised hand sweeping first to the left then to the right (left-handed, remember, these little spontaneous things will always give a man away; but Eglon hasn't noticed it, thank goodness) and then back to the king. "It's from God, sir. And it's for you alone."

It was perfect. Magnificent. On the stage it would have brought every member of the crowd right to the edge of his chair. On the screen it would have made me remember to make a note of the producer's name. Faultless.

Eglon paused nearly twenty seconds. For Ehud an absolute age must have stood still as those moments passed, but his eyes and his attention did not falter by the tiniest flickering shadow of movement.

"Leave us." Eglon's words and single gesture from one bloated jewel-encrusted hand brought instant action. The Moabite servants bowed and silently slipped out of the room. Only Eglon, huge mountainous Eglon still reclining back in his padded chair, and Ehud, left-handed Ehud kneeling on his left knee with that so-business like little dagger still strapped to his right thigh, remaining.

And the distance is still not quite right. It will take both a lunge and a step to reach Eglon with the sword. About two seconds too much time is needed, it's just not right, even now!

And Ehud hasn't moved. Not a fraction of an inch. His voice is still a hoarse whisper, as with downcast eyes he speaks. "Yes, sir, it's from God. I had to come and tell you."

"Speak up, man! I can't properly hear you. Tell me, what is it the gods want me to know?"

Was it greed? Was it conceit? Was it something more than greed, something greater than conceit? Was it perhaps fear, the fear man always has when finally confronted by his God? Was it this that swept his caution aside? Perhaps that is the real answer, perhaps that properly explains why his two hands gripped the arms of his chair so strongly, why there was that sudden heave as he raised his whole lumbering bulk on to feet that could just barely carry him—and there he was, half-standing, just above Ehud, just that half pace closer that Ehud needed.

A sudden flash, a slight hiss of breath as the Benjamite springs, a single muffled gasp from the stricken king, and it's over. Eglon is dead. Collapsed in a ghastly mountain of fat-enveloped flesh.

No turmoil, no thrashing and pounding of fisticuffs and smashing of balsa-wood furniture in the way the Hollywood westerns conclude. Just sudden, instant death. Hardly a sound. Nothing to show what happened. Even the dagger isn't to be seen now. Eglon has the dagger Ehud came to give to him. Ehud has completed his mission. The dagger has disappeared completely into the great belly of the Moabite king, the flesh has closed over blade and haft alike. Eglon now has it! Only the small trickle of blood and the larger stream of bowel contents give out the secret at all. That and the stench that now no nostril could mistake. Eglon is dead.

But the stillness of death lasts only a moment, and then Ehud is on his feet. He's stepping behind the screens and out into the private way of retreat that Eglon had prepared for his own personal comfort, and Ehud is gone. Gone past the guards, slipping clean away, running at last down the

Gilgal road, past the Sculptured Stones, up into the hills and home ...

"Deal me out, Mesha. I'm broke. You've skinned me dry, blast you."

The guard tossed down the dice he had been holding and stretched his arms as he clambered to his feet.

"Aw, don't give up now, Seraph. Your luck will come back. Mine has!" And the Moabite opposite him began to flick the pile of bone counters in front of him into a leather purse he had materialised from under his cloak. "Sure, it's only a matter of time and you'll be in the money again."

"Yes, Seraph. That's right. And even if you are broke, what of it? Why not ask Eglon for a loan? He's loaded! And this Ehud bloke must have been giving him all the low-down in the world, they've been nattering away so long. It's hours now, they must have talked their throats dry."

"Listen, you fellows. I'm worried. I wonder if it's really OK. I've never known Eglon go as long as this without calling for drinks, it just doesn't seem right to me."

"Yeah, but what can we do?"

"Oh, forget it, fellows. Let's get on with the game. My luck's in, and I want to try and get back all that dough you tore off me two days ago. Zuk, it's your deal."

"Wait a minute. I think Ithrah's right. We ought to try and find out whether the old man is all right."

"Ha! How dumb can you get! You want to burst in and say, 'Oh, Eglon, excuse me, sir, but I thought I'd just pop in and see that you are managing comfortably.' Listen, stupid: one fellow did that about three years ago, walked straight into the room when Eglon was in his little toilet. Boy, oh boy! I still wake up at night dreaming about that wretch. I've never seen anything like it. Eglon was so angry I thought he'd die. He was as white as a piece of alabaster. His eyes were just tiny little slits. His voice was so soft it was absolutely creepy. 'Tie him up.' That was all he said. Then, 'Cut out his tongue.' Quiet, slow, simple like that. 'Cut out his tongue.' It was Bek who had to do it, and Bek

had been a mate of his. And Bek's knife was blunt, and
Eglon just whispered 'Right out. Cut it right out.' And then
as we carried the poor beggar out Eglon said, 'Bring him
back tomorrow and we'll cut off his hands. Then the next
day we'll cut off his feet.' But he was lucky in the end—
he died that same day. I've never seen so much blood come
from one fellow." He stopped and wiped his sleeve across
his so-damp forehead. "Sure, you burst in on him if you
like, but not with me, thank you. Count me right out. I'm
not that crazy."

And so it was that the day was almost run clean out before
Eglon was found. Before the fearful guards at last realised
that the king's insistence for privacy in his physiological
excretory processes was perhaps making them forgetful of
the king's safety overall.

And what scenario, from Hollywood or Ealing or even
Stratford-upon-Avon itself, could depict the sheer horror of
that moment. That moment when at last the door was flung
open and the ashen faces and starting eyeballs of the already
fear-filled guards saw the great hulk of Eglon, heard the
buzzing of the thick-gathering flies, smelt the noisome foulness of the spilt death that had trickled out beside the haft
of the buried sword.

And the dismay of the guards became the terror of all
Moab, as the cheering Israelites came tumbling down the
hill-slopes with left-handed Ehud at their head. Eglon, fat
Eglon, was dead. Moab, the tyranny of Moab, was at an end.
God had saved His people.

"The Israelites did what was wrong in the eyes of the
Lord, and because of this he roused Eglon king of Moab
against Israel ... When they cried to the Lord for help, he
raised up a man to deliver them, Ehud ... Thus Moab on that
day became subject to Israel, and the land was at peace ..."

Hmmmm. Quite a story, isn't it? I warned you, you may
remember. I told you that these stories might be crude and
sordid and just plain human.

Oh, I had to guess a bit here and there. I guessed that

bit about the protocol and the ritual in Eglon's presence:
the record tells us quite clearly that the tribute was actually
paid out in Eglon's view, but Eglon was Eglon, I had no
question in my mind about guessing that it all took place in
Moab itself and not in Jericho, the City of Palms, and that
it would be certain to take place in that lovely rooftop arbour
of his. Those were guesses and they may be wrong, but that
doesn't matter, and they are not absurdly wrong. And I had
to imagine some parts, too. I had to imagine something
really gruesome about Eglon, gruesome enough to keep those
guards hanging around outside the door of his roof-chamber
until "they were ashamed to delay any longer". Sure, I
imagined those details, and I make no apology for imagining
them, for I know enough about people to know that something very, very like that must have been going on. So that
I make no apology for that somewhat lewd insistence on the
significance of that private toilet—I know that I am not
placing too much emphasis on that. The extreme sensitivity
of a gross freak of a man like Eglon will drive him to astonishing lengths to hide his disgusting physical deformity. No,
I'm not making too much of that—the whole story hangs
on that toilet.

For the Hebrew historian has the most disarmingly casual
way of hiding his headlines, a technique that carries a pungent emphasis to the reader who understands that writing
method, but to the modern westerner, accustomed to seeing
every single highlight of the story spread clean across the
page in huge eye-catching 72-point type, it does indeed
need more imagining.

But I'm not writing as a historian. Still less as a bio-
grapher. Least of all as a mere storyteller. And when I say
that the story of Eglon and Ehud is quite a story, I mean
it is quite a story in more ways than being just a yarn or
biography or bit of history. For I am writing as one whose
business is with people; but more still as one who claims
to have found some of life's real answers. I claim to have
met God: more correctly, that God has met me. And that
it is from Him that this real meaning has come. And that

is what makes this quite a story.

For all this is planned. God says He did it. "The Lord roused Eglon king of Moab against Israel." That's what God has written in His account. Eighteen years, that went on, with God rousing Eglon against the Israelites. And then God says that He was responsible for Ehud. "The Lord raised up a man to deliver them, Ehud son of Gera, the Benjamite, who was left-handed." You see what I mean? Ehud was left-handed, and that's why I felt it was quite important to imagine some pattern of ceremony that would need a man to be left-handed if he was going to dig a knife into Eglon. And left-handedness is something you are born with. It's in your genes. It needs a left-handed ancestor. (We'll see later that Benjamin was not a bit short of left-handed men!) And you can't become left-handed just because you get arthritis in your right hand. In fact you can't become left-handed even if you chop your right hand clean off. It's in the brain. It's innate. God arranged that. God planned that.

Now you see why this is quite a story. Because God says it is His story. It is His work. His plan and activity. And now perhaps you see, also, why some people don't like the Book of Judges. Some people think the Bible ought to be a pleasant sort of children's book to teach the kiddies to be nice little girls and boys because God loves nice little girls and boys so run along and play now dear children and be sweet to each other and don't play rough games or use rude words and always say please and thank you. Sure, you can see why some people are unhappy about the Book of Judges, and why they are so bothered to find something that says so bluntly that God is not just what they have always thought He ought to be, that God is not made in the image they have built for Him.

For God says, in this so-disturbing story, that He can't be measured by the measure of man's limitations. It is for us to discover what He says He in fact is like, to discover that He is as great as this.

Now I did say in the Prologue to this book that I don't want to stop and debate these issues, however worthy they are of such debate. But I do most certainly want to insist that the truth still stands—God is *God*, and this is still His world.

That bitter, oppressive tyranny of the greedy monster, Eglon, was not just fate, mere bad luck, simply the way life goes and it's all nice and easy for the fortunate few who get the social breaks and make the A-grades and just one heck of a hateful time for the poor devil who gets caught up in the mess and who gets nailed to the wall in the final show-down—no, it's not merely that. Sure, it may be all of that, and is all that. But, God is insisting, it is not just that. It is also meaning. It is purpose. It is intention. For it is God.

And that is why this story cannot be omitted from any meaningful understanding of the Book of Judges. Because it is the story which insists so dramatically, and so dogmatically, that even in encounters as sordid and crude and hate-filled as this, we must still be reminded that this is God, that in awe-full truth, God is *God*.

For in the four succeeding stories, in these so-personal experiences of Barak, Gideon, Jephthah and of Samson, this truth is never to be forgotten. Indeed, in your own story just as in mine, the full meaning of any and of all happenings, good or bad, pleasant or unpleasant, successful or unsuccessful—always—it is God. In the actual life-and-death struggle that really constitutes human existence—it is there, and it is then, in every development and in every detail, that God is meeting with man. For then we may learn how utterly God may really be seen to be, how completely God is *God*.

BARAK

The Canaanites* were just about at their heyday. Their civilisation was now over a thousand years old, and their tiny piece of country had that richness and fame and culture that only centuries can provide. It wasn't just their wealth, it was the trimmings to their wealth.

So that to the hill-people looking down on their lowland luxury and their rich coastal trade it was an almost fairyland mixture of pleasure and plenty. Zebulun and Naphtali, those were the tribes to which most of these hill-people belonged. And Zebulun and Naphtali are the tribes we are concerned with now.

It was the same old impasse all over again: the call of God to remain separate and distinct and un-mixed up with all the religion and materialism on these surrounding nations —and the simple human desire for comfort, convenience and cash.

And it was Jabin who clamped down on it all. Jabin, the Canaanite king. Jabin, backed up by Sisera, his commander-in-chief. Yes, backed up is the right word, for Sisera was himself backed up by no less than nine hundred chariots. And what's more, it was nine hundred *iron* chariots. The world's number one armoured division—that's what Sisera was backed up by.

Jabin changed it all and that's for sure. Jabin plus Sisera

* This particular part of Canaan is the part that will become Phoenicia in about another hundred years. It is the tiny piece of coastland and river flat that today runs up and down the coast in the region of Tripoli, and their holding took in the river valley there. But the all-important thing about this people lies in their possession of the Hittite secret of iron-making—the most fabulous, man-devouring metal man has ever had in his hands to help him to kill his neighbour—that, they have got.

plus nine hundred iron chariots.

Now I'm not making any silly mistakes about those chariots. I know quite well that they weren't the diesel-engined, crawler-tracked, bullet-proof, multi-cannon-powered monsters that the late twentieth century chooses for its armoured divisions. No, nothing like that. But to the poor, starving, half-naked, unarmed Zebulunites and Naphtalites any difference was of no real distinction at all. If you were hoping to sneak down into Hazor or into Kedesh or into Harosheth or into any other Canaanite city, those chariots were all the dissuasion you would need. For those chariots each carried three fighting men, armed to the teeth; and the chariots were drawn by horses, those great big prancing, leaping, dashing animals that the Hyksos people had only recently brought over from the steppe-lands away up to their north-east; and, most fearsome of all, the chariots were framed and armed with iron, that wickedly strong flesh-fearing metal that the Hittites had learned to draw out of the very ores in the ground. And now the Canaanites, sitting there so prettily on the main trade route of this world, had bought up the Hyksos horses, had captured the Hittite iron-making secret, had perfected the war-chariot—and now what hope in the world had a poor Naphtalite of sneaking down into that country and coming as a refugee?

Of course there were a few—a very few—who did it. But they did it differently. They did it by treaty, they really did it by treason. For there will always be a few people, in London and in Berlin, in New York and in Moscow, in Sydney and in Peking, who will do that. Defect. Sell out. Do a little personal deal. Double talk.

Like Heber. Heber was really a Kenite. The Kenites were Arabs, but they were Arabs who had joined Moses nearly a hundred years before (Moses' wife was an Arab) and their descendants, the Kenites, had tagged along with the Israelites ever since. But not Heber. Heber had sold out. He had a nice little personal arrangement with Jabin, and Jabin had allowed him to set up his tent at a place called Za-anannim, just a couple of miles outside Kedesh itself. And Heber could slip out of bed in the morning and stand at the door of his tent and stretch his arms and blink the sleep out of his eyes as the slanting rays of the rising sun came glinting in on his right. For there, just there below him, lay the rich river flat of Megiddo itself. That lush valley of Jezreel that filled the Canaanite larder with such lavish plenty. And Heber could yawn his welcome to the new day, because he would be sharing it with his colleague, Jabin. Heber was playing it by ear, but the tune was coming out pretty much on key.

Yes, lucky Heber. Lucky few who could do this sort of deal with Jabin, especially now that Jabin was backed up by Sisera backed up by nine hundred chariots. Lucky few indeed.

But tough luck for the poor devils who didn't have it all tied up with Jabin. Those miserable rats were in trouble, plenty of trouble. Lots of them, there were. Hundreds, thousands.

Like Barak. Barak was there too, only a couple of miles from Heber, but a couple of very, very important miles. Because they were a couple of miles up the steep slopes of the craggy hills, and that meant a couple of miles just out of the reach of those deadly chariots. Sure, a couple of very valuable miles! But also a couple of miles further from those rich Canaanite supply lines. A couple of teasing, taunting miles if ever there were.

There Barak was, as close as all that to danger; yet as far as that from all the tasty goodies.

And I don't know what would have happened, I can't even guess what might have happened, if this had all been left entirely alone, just to work itself out. But the simple truth is that God doesn't ever leave men alone. He never leaves things simply to work themselves out. God is always controlling, He is always involved. And God sent a message to Barak.

Now the message didn't come in a visionary sort of trance or anything exotic like that. Not that God can't and may not at rare times speak to a man like that. God speaks just

how and where and when He plans. But not to Barak. God
didn't speak to Barak like that.

The message came from away down in the south, from
Bethel. It called Barak down there. Quickly. *Pronto. Instanter.
Summa cum celeritate*, if I remember my earliest Latin
phrases correctly. Bethel was about fifty miles away, one
very dickens of a long way away. For it was not fifty miles
of bitumenised road and motor transport. It was fifty miles
of hill country and mountain tracks and danger from ambush
and brigandry. But the message was from God, and Barak
just went.

Yes, God had sent it. And even though it may not have
arrived in the pre-breakfast mail one day, it still came in the
form of a note. A note from a woman. God is always doing
that sort of thing. Sending messages to people, writing official notes to people, typing out instructions to people. And
nearly always God does this by getting some person or
other to speak the actual words, to take pen and ink and
do the writing, to sit down and punch the keys of the type-
writer. But remember, it is God who really does it. Always
God.

The woman was Deborah, and Deborah was the
"prophetess" of the Israelite people at that time. Later
prophets used to come around the country and look after
their people's affairs at close-up, first hand. But Deborah was
a woman and she did it differently. She just stayed at home
and sent for Barak.

My, how I would love to have a video-tape of that meeting! I am absolutely certain I know how Barak felt. I don't
think there is any single character in the whole of Scripture
who is as direct and straightforward and uncomplicated as
Barak. (And I don't know any Bible character whose spiritual
experience I would more gladly share than the very same
Barak!)

If Barak had been a great big, tough, heavy-fisted, loud-
voiced he-man with long black hair all over his chest, who
twisted iron bars in his bare fists and lit safety matches with
a flick of his thumb and played lock forward in the rugby

scrum—then I don't think Deborah would have had the nerve to summon him as tersely as this. No, I think she would have up-skirts and gone off to meet him in his own power-packed territory. And what is more, I don't think a strongarm tough guy like that would have lifted a single shoe-strap to step one pace to meet a mere dame like that.

But Barak was just Barak, a simple ordinary run-of-the-mill average anybody, that's all he was, and he came struggling across the lousy mountain road to her. Barak was like that.

Now if this page is being read by a charming lady whose name is Deborah, then don't blame me. If you are a sweet little cutie, all femininity and light laughter, it's certainly not my fault. I didn't invent the name, and I certainly didn't give it to you. What's more, it's a million to one your mum and dad never bothered to read this story of the original Deborah, or they could never possibly have dropped down into the bottom of that trap.

Deborah was the very opposite to Barak. She was tough. She was flint. She was the Boadicea of Israel. You just wait till you come to the end of this story. Fancy being Lappidoth, Deborah's husband!

Barak stood there stunned. Absolutely groggy.

When he first set out on his journey he may well have been a bit nervous, as any ordinary simple man might be. That's understandable and reasonable. Getting hauled up to Bethel like that would make any fellow feel like that. A sort of Buckingham Palace panic. If the Americans changed their practices and got women presidents, you could call it the White House Blue Funk. Barak had that, a proper and reasonable dose of that, but nothing else. Just good respectable nerves.

But now he was dazed. His slightly knocking knees were so flabby that they couldn't even shake at all. The little quiver of lip had given way to a gaping paralytic leer.

For he had only just arrived, had only just announced who he was, when Deborah had begun to flatten him. "Ho,

Ho, Barak!" she boomed. "Splendid of you. Your big
moment, Barak! The absolute chance of a lifetime. Listen:
God wants you to collect up ten thousand men from the
tribe of Naphtali and from the tribe of Zebulun. Get them
all together with your own local chaps, up on the top of
Mount Tabor. What do you think of that?"

She paused to gather breath and to let this sink in. Sink in
is the word! It sank in, for sure. Sank right down into the
bottom of his very bones. Barak wasn't a mind reader, but
he knew in a flash what she meant. She meant him to get
an army together, and muster his troops up on Tabor. But
why Mount Tabor? Tabor, of all places! For that was the
mountain peak on the opposite side of the Megiddo Valley,
directly across the plain from his own home near Kedesh.
Right up there where Sisera would see every single man on
it.

Barak got the message. And Deborah saw that Barak had
got the message. That tensing of muscle, that stiffening of
stance—Deborah saw that she had got through to Barak.
But what she didn't even guess was what Barak thought of
the message. Barak's thoughts were simple. Very simple.
Simple and sensible and normal and rational and prudent
and everything else that any ordinary average man would
think about a crack-pot scheme like this. Only a dame could
cook up an idea as crazy as this. Ten thousand men—that's
a lot of men. And on Mount Tabor—that's right in the
front of the Megiddo stage, Sisera, with his nine hundred
iron chariots and all his beautiful armour and weapons and
big prancing horses watching every tiny detail of it.

Yes. That's what Barak thought and that's certainly the
way I would have thought, too. But Deborah wasn't like
that, she didn't for a moment realise what he was thinking.
As she saw the quick narrowing of eyelids and pursing of
lips she completely misunderstood what was in his mind.

"Barak," she burst out again, "don't look so worried.
You'll have no trouble with Sisera. God will draw him. He
won't try and escape you. God will see to that!" And she
stamped her $7\frac{1}{2}$EE sandal on the dusty ground as she simply

spat out his name again. "Sisera! That wretch of an army
general!" And she swung back the sleeve of her robe in a
magnificent gesture of defiance. "He won't be able to dodge
you, Barak. God will see to that. You collect up those men
and take them down on to the banks of the Kishon River and
God will see to it that Sisera will be right there with all his
troops and every chariot he possesses. And 'they're yours
Barak. Just for the taking. God will hand the whole lot
over to you!"

Mad! That's what Deborah must have been. Crazy.
Absolutely off her rocker. The average man is a bit sus-
picious of women in matters of politics and affairs. That's
not only because of prejudice and male ego. It's also because
he has probably been on a committee, in a business meeting,
something like that, when a woman has suddenly come out
with some wildcat scheme that's going to land them thousands
of dollars in the red or take up all their leisure time for
months or goodness knows what. Sure, that's normal, that's
woman.

But did you ever hear of anything just as completely potty
as this? Collect up some untrained, unarmed, unkempt hill-
billies on a mountain top, where they might perhaps be
safe, and then deliberately stroll down on to the nice smooth,
level river flats to tackle the greatest armoured task force
the world had ever seen. Not a tree for camouflage, not a
single rocky outcrop, even, to hide behind.

Mad! I'll say she must be mad. But that's not the really
mad bit. Crazy lunatics like that turn up now and again,
but that's not what jolted poor Barak so hard. No, it was
that "draw him" bit. That utterly incredible idea that he
(Barak) was a bit worried because Sisera might try and
dodge him. She really thought he was scared that Sisera
might not turn up. That Sisera might sneak off in terror.
And that then Barak's men might not get the chance to do
them over. Yes, that was what she was thinking. That's how
her brain worked. That's how absolutely incredibly, awfully,
unbelievably way-out she was! Here, she is saying, dear
little fly, you just jump into that web. Right into the middle,

little fly, and I promise you that the nasty big black spider
will come out. The spider won't try to get away. And Micky,
you cute wee mouse, you; I've found a lovely big cage full
of cats for you to capture. Beautiful sleek tabbies and Manxes
and Persians, all about a thousand times as big as you. Nice
little Micky, just spring in through the bars of the cage—
you're tiny enough to fit through the cracks—and they're
yours. They can't get out, Micky, they won't even try to
get away from you.

I must confess that every time I think of this little episode
there is a chuckle bursting up inside me. Sometimes even a
genuinely irreverent guffaw. That "I will draw Sisera" bit.
I can't think of anything in Thackeray, Gilbert and Sullivan
or P. G. Wodehouse himself, that can beat that for sheer
farce! And even as I throw my head back to burst out laughing I feel the tight twist inside me that reminds me of the
staring, white-faced tragedy that swept over Barak. Sure,
it's as funny as can be, if you're three thousand years from
it. But to the man in the middle, the poor clot who has to
go and be the bunny, who has to be the bait in the trap, it's
just too un-funny for words.

For Deborah wasn't just mad. She wasn't simply stupid.
She wasn't merely the unpredictable, irrational, altogether
intuitive creature that is woman—she was the prophetess.
She was the messenger of God. This absurdly ridiculous
fly-chase-spider, mouse-attack-cat scheme wasn't only hers,
it was God's!

So that I always wonder how it was that Barak managed
to answer Deborah. How he got the nerve and strength to
make his so-parched lips move to frame any words at all.
I've never wondered how he thought up what to say—he
didn't! A man just clobbered with that sort of sledge-hammer
doesn't come back with some sparkling bit of repartee, some
Churchillian turn of eloquence. I know I just couldn't have
said a single word.

But Barak's answer came, and it told his feelings and his
mind just as surely as a most carefully reasoned treatise.

"Deborah," he croaked in a voice that was so nearly beyond speech, "if you go with me, I'll go. But if you won't go with me, I won't go."

Barak, you're magnificent. Just tremendous! No wonder God has kept your story in His Book. No wonder your name is in that most celebrated Honours List ever to be announced: that Order of Merit membership roll preserved for us in the eleventh chapter of the Epistle to the Hebrews. Barak, even as your jaw sagged and your eyeballs glazed over, you had got it right. "Deborah, if you go with me, I'll go. But if you won't go with me, I won't go." But that wasn't really it, was it, Barak? It wasn't really Deborah, it was in fact God you were talking to—Deborah was only the prophetess, she was merely the divine messenger, she was just the mouth-piece. But you were answering God: "God," you were saying, "this all sounds far too mad to be true. Just crazy. But if You come along, then I'll be in it. No matter how ridiculous it all seems. But not on my own. Not without You, God."

Barak, no wonder God has put you on His list. K.O.'d and every single puff of wind knocked clean out of you, you're still saying, "God, I'm still with You, and with You alone. Not me. Just You, and me with You."

And I take a deep breath to burst into a loud and excited cheer. But I can't. Because Deborah stops me. "Barak," she says, "that's splendid. I'll certainly be there. You won't catch me missing this!" And I'm wondering how a Hollywood writer or impresario would script this—would he have Deborah (about 5′ 11″) throw her arms around the neck of Barak (about 5′ 8″) and hug him?

But it's not Hollywood, it's Bethel, 1200 B.C. And Deborah is not a celluloid star, she's poor Lappidoth's wife, and no hugging and arms around neck at all. Just an icy, sharp "Barak, let's get this straight. You're only playing a bit part. No starring role, my man. Not for you. The bright lights and the ticker-tape will all go to a woman. God is going to see to it that a women gets Sisera. Come on, now, let's go."

And she turned on her heel and strode off ahead of him, up the road to Kedesh ...

When war was looming large on the horizons of Europe in the late thirties, our R.A.A.F. decided to bestir itself. Australia set herself up as a war-plane manufacturer. Not Spitfires or Hurricanes or Wellingtons from Britain, or even imitation Stukas or Messerschmidts or Heinkels from Germany. No, our very own plane, we announced, that's what we would make, just the plane for Australia's needs: the Wirraway.

And it was in a newsreel theatre that I saw the film of the first Wirraway coming off the assembly line. (I forget how many weeks it took for the next one to follow!) But we were in real business, the commentator told us, our defences were beginning to take meaningful shape. And can I ever forget the let-down feeling that sagged down into my very stomach as this pathetic little plane fluttered into the skies with its 180 m.p.h. maximum and its two machine-guns firing through the props. This was still a few short years before Darwin. Darwin, where we paid a bitterly high price for such wanton pride, as our boys took those same wretched Wirraways into the fire-line of the attacking Japanese Zeros. No, as I watched that newsreel, I didn't know what was going to happen in Darwin; but I did know enough to realise that something like that could happen. And even as I thought this, as the let-down anti-climax of it struck me so forcibly, the scene changed.

And what a change! For now on the screen it was Berlin, it was Hitler. The camera was this time panning that vast parade ground with its endless sea of troops, of tanks, of power unlimited, of the might that was Hitler's Germany. And my thoughts flashed back to that single sputtering Wirraway, our Aussie answer to the Axis might. And I sat there and watched: the troops marching wave up on wave upon wave, millions, it seemed; and the tanks rolling, thundering past in hundreds, in thousands; and the Führer's voice rising to a frenzy of passion and hate—when suddenly the screen was blacked out and the little theatre was choked with a deafening roar that even Hitler could not match. It was the Luftwaffe. It was the German Air Force. It was the thundering flash of the low-flying air squadrons, telling the world of their power, their speed, their might.

And Sisera did the same. Three thousand years before Hitler, Sisera did exactly the same thing. As news came through to him from his agents, as his under-cover men moved among the Israelites, in whispered the news. "Barak is up to something." "Barak should be watched." "Barak's collecting a lot of men." "It looks as though Barak is probably only the front man." (This, I think, from Heber the Kenite. He lived only a mile or two from Barak, he was pretty close to the heart of the scheme, the miserable fifth-column rat.). "He's really a pretty ordinary little yokel, but he's under the absolute thumb of a great big lanky Amazon of a wild-eyed dame called Deborah. She's probably the power behind all the scenes—but Barak's the one to keep an eye on." "Best part of ten thousand, that's my estimate. Ragged, useless collection of no-hopers, that's all you could call them, but they're still streaming in. You'd better set up a bit of counter-propaganda. I'd break this up, if I were you."

And I can hear in my imagination the click of heels and the tramp of jack-boots and the staccato gutterals of barked-out commands—and Sisera is moving. Moving out into the open. Out into the wide, rolling grasslands and river flats on the floor of the valley. Out into that immense parade ground, spread out so clearly at the very foot of the hills. Watched, he is so sure, by every single eye up there above him. Yes, watched by the twenty thousand eyes of the ten thousand men with Barak on Mount Tabor.

Did Hitler read the Book of Judges? Did Hitler simply lift a leaf from Sisera's copybook? Or is this the measure of the arrogance and the pride and the aggression that is just the biological nature of man? I can only guess, and you can only guess. But what nobody need guess is what it looked like to that puny little force of men up on the hilltop. You're not guessing at all when you think how they felt. I felt the same, that day in the news-theatre in Sydney; and I was eleven thousand miles from Berlin.

No, it's no guessing matter. As wave after wave of chariots flashed up and down the valley, as column joined column and formed into thundering blocks of solid power, as manoeuvre followed manoeuvre—no, you're not guessing. Only the hills kept them alive: that's what those men up there knew. The rocks and the cliff-faces and the ravines and the bouldered watercourses—this was their sole hope of life. But down there, down on the flats and the level ground and the plains—death. Horrible, mangling, bloody death! That's no place for them to fight, that's the one place to stay out of.

And Sisera saw that. That's why he did it. Sure, he knew that. And I know that, and you know that, and every single man Jack of the ten thousand of them knew that.

But Deborah did not know that. Only Deborah didn't know. That crazy, dumb, impossible dame just didn't know anything at all. She wasn't "solid ivory, from the occiput to the frontal bone" like one of P. G. Wodehouse's characters; she was just woolly. Her head wasn't full of dull, heavy, useless stuff like concrete or granite; her head was bursting with loose, fluffy, flyaway, gossamer stuff like cotton wool. Gun-cotton wool, if that's really what I mean, because it was liable to explode into some wild-eyed nonsensical absurdity at any single moment.

And the moment came. She exploded. The whole head-full of craziness went up in one single shattering bang!

"Barak!" she exclaimed, "today!"

Barak was getting more used to her, I'm sure he was learning just what allowances he had to make for her, but this beat him. I'd be the same. If somebody came up to me one morning and clapped me over the shoulder and exclaimed in a rather wild-sounding voice, "John, today!", I'd be the same. Sure, I'd say to myself quickly, "today" is a noun. What is it doing? What is it supposed to be?

Lovely clear morning, can't be the weather he means. Oh,
April 22nd—no, not our wedding anniversary or anybody's
birthday. I must be a bit dumb. Today what? I don't get it.

And Barak looked round, too. It was a glorious morning,
a bit warmer than usual, even for that part of the world,
but he couldn't see what about today. A quick glance down
on to the plains—but, no, Sisera hadn't packed up, everything looked just as hopeless as any other day looked hopeless. Today what?

But Deborah wasn't asking him. She was telling him.

"Barak, don't just stand there. Today's your big day.
Quick! On your way. Get cracking. Today God is going to
deliver Sisera and his men into your hand. Snap into it,
man! God will be there ahead of you. Down you go!"

I know why Barak's name is on that Honours Roll. Why
his name is in that famous chapter in the letter to the
Hebrews. "So Barak came charging down from Mount Tabor
with ten thousand men at his back." That is why. I just
know in my heart that if God told me to do that I'd be
arguing it out with Him still, and I'd spend the whole of the
first day arguing just why it should be today and not
tomorrow. And God just said, "Up, this is the day."

I'm not squeamish at the sight of blood. You can't buy
into medical practice and spend thousands of mornings in
operating theatres and still find your stomach turning over
because somebody is bleeding. No. But I am concerned for
people, people are my business, and the thought of Barak
just dashing down from Mount Tabor with his pitiful bare-
foot followers is enough to fill my very heart with lead. I
feel I want to shut the book and just pretend I can't see. I
don't even want to read about it. As the Israelites come
within charging range of those fearsome chariots, as the
horses leap into action, as the steel slashes into puny flesh—
I can't stand it. Oh, God, I say, as I clasp my hands over
already tight-shut eyes, Your purposes are bigger than life
because they are so much greater than death. And Barak's

Your man, and even if it requires this suicide programme to bring it about, I'm not questioning for a single moment Your right to do it this way. I know You well enough, now, trust You well enough, now, not to doubt that again.

But God, must I watch it happen? Must I open my eyes and just gape like a blood-lusting spectator at the arena, as men go down to their violent death? Will I learn anything more just by staring at it?

And the cold heaviness within me is matched by a sudden chill in the air around me. The day that had started out so over-warm and still is suddenly stirred by an icy gust that matched the event itself. And the sudden personal discomfort makes me forget my concern for Barak and his men, and I open my eyes and move a hand to throw a jacket round my shoulders. Hmmm, winter soon, I'm saying. And the page is open, open right there in front of me, and I just glance at it. And I read ...

"The Lord put Sisera to rout with all his chariots and his army before Barak's onslaught; but Sisera himself dismounted from his chariot and fled on foot. Barak pursued the chariots and the army as far as Harosheth, and the whole army was put to the sword and perished; not a man was left alive. Meanwhile Sisera fled on foot ..."

That's word for word. I am quoting from the New English Bible, and that's exactly as they have it there. I notice that there are two references to Sisera getting away on foot—that seems to be important enough to make the Hebrew writer repeat himself, and that is not his common way of reporting, to be sure. But there's nothing else about it that says anything at all about what has actually been going on. Not a word. Just that rather laconic casualness that I now realise is the signal to look more carefully and discover the hidden headline—but in this case there is not even a hidden syllable, let alone a whole headline.

Hey, wait a minute, I yell. Not so fast. Here I was shutting my eyes so as not to see the horrible ghastly massacre of those half-naked hill-people under the iron-banded wheels of all those chariots, and all you say is that the Canaanite

army was completely wiped out. Annihilated. All strewn
about the place, right over the whole valley floor, bodies
and horses and ironmongery, to the very gates of Harosheth
itself. Listen! I'm used to this. I know! I'm not as simple
and green as all that. No, sir! Through the whole of the
war years I used to hear the war bulletins from the B.B.C.,
and I know what's what. Even the fantasy of the Battle of
Britain—you know, that "Ten Spitfires engaged an estimated
force of sixty enemy bombers and their cover of twenty
fighters. Twelve bombers were destroyed, eighteen damaged,
and at least eleven fighters brought down. Two of our aircraft were lost and three are missing. One of our pilots
parachuted to safety." Sure, I'm brought up on that sort
of reporting, sometimes true, sometimes partly true, sometimes as phoney as can be. But not what you are saying.
That's like saying: "Two R.A.A.F. flight-sergeants today
attacked a squadron of sixty Zeros. The sergeants were
repairing their Wirraways with sticky tape and scrap fencing-
wire when the air-raid siren sounded. Without waiting even
to top up their fuel tanks the two Australians took to the
air and went to the attack. Twenty-nine Zeros are known to
have crashed, and the others were all damaged. It is unlikely
that any will be able to return to base. One Wirraway was
badly damaged when a tyre burst on landing. The pilot is
unhurt. The other aircraft has several bullet holes in the
fuselage, but some of these are likely to be old holes waiting
repair after previous encounters."

But the historian doesn't answer me. My taunts and jeers
pass unheeded. I'm wasting my breath.

For the writer of the Book of Judges is flat out following
Sisera, who fled away on foot. The commander-in-chief
is dashing off for his life, running back into the hill country
itself, so desperately pressed now to escape. And I give a
great bellow of laughter as I think of the sheer absurdity of
this—Sisera, on foot! How did he come to be the only one
to get away? Was he like Gilbert's Duke of Plazo Toro, who
"led his regiment from behind, he found it less exciting"?

But I can't stop for breath, not even for another chuckle,

for Sisera is dashing up the hills as if chased by every devil in hell, there is panic driving him, the same panic that he has so often seen on the faces of those other poor devils he has trampled under the wheels of his famous chariots.

But not aimlessly. Not stupidly. Sisera is running, running for his life, but he knows where he's going. He's making for Heber's place, Heber the Kenite, the local Israelite Quisling who is on Jabin's pay roll. He'll be safe there. Hole up in Heber's tent and nobody would ever think of looking for him there. Commander-in-Chief of all Canaan, running away into the heart of the hill country—sure, he'd be utterly safe, and Heber could get him away back to Kedesh when the hue and cry died down.

And he's made it. He's safe. It's Heber's tent. And Sisera falls on his face and gasps for the breath that seems so scarcely to fill his lungs. His whole body is trembling from terror and exhaustion, but he's safe. Heber's place.

And there, running lightly over to him to help him, to lift him to his feet, to wipe away the sweat that is filling his eyes and the blood-flecked spittle that is trickling out of the corner of his mouth, is Jaël, Heber's wife. Pretty little thing, Sisera notices, but he's not really interested in pretty little things just now. He's done. He needs help. And she's there to help him, she's Heber's wife, she'll look after him. ·

"Here you are, Lord Sisera. Come along in. Do let me help you, sir. You're right now, your Lordship, you're safe." And she half supported, half led him into the tent, on to the soft sheep-skin rug that served for the mattress and couch.

"Please." He could only gasp. "Please—a drink. Water. Just a drink. Please. Thirsty. A drink of water."

Jael bowed and smiled her sympathy. Her light feet tripped away to the far corner of the tent. Not to bring him water, but to bring him milk. Yoghurt, the thick curdled milk that was such luxury in their poverty-pressed economy.

And Sisera drank, a mere sip at first, the slight bitterness of the yoghurt meeting the dust and dryness of his palate in choking impact. Then more freely. Then gulping it down,

in the overwhelming sense of relief that his safety now sup-
plied to him. Heber's home. He is safe. And his head
slipped back on to the couch, her light fingers and soft touch
now drew a coverlet over him, he could sleep.

"Listen!" The sudden imperiousness of years of domination and leadership was back for just a moment. "Stand
guard. Stand at the door of the tent. If anybody comes, don't
open it. Don't say I'm here. Just say there's nobody home."

Sisera, the man who just a few short hours ago was the
leader of the greatest fighting unit the world had ever seen,
was asleep. Asleep in a humble goat's hair tent, hiding up
in hostile enemy country, guarded by a single hill-people
housewife! Asleep. Safe.

"But Jael, Heber's wife, took a tent-peg, picked up a
hammer, crept up to him, and drove the peg into his skull
as he lay sound asleep. His brains oozed out on the ground,
his limbs twitched, and he died."

I've just had a cup of coffee. I needed it. I'm not sure
that one is enough. Not sure that even coffee is enough.
There is a slightly cotton wool sort of buzzing in my temples,
a symptom patients talk about at times and don't seem to
be able to describe very clearly. I can't either. Not after a
story like that.

I don't quite know what to do. Or what to say. That's
the story as I read it. That's the end. That's all there is.
Finis. Barak has just arrived at Heber's place. He is striding up to Jael. Jael is going out to meet him, she's greeting
him. Listen: " 'Come, I will show you the man you are looking for.' He went in with her, and there was Sisera lying
dead with the tent-peg in his skull."

That's it. That's all. One tent-peg through a man's head
is all he ever gets. Curtain. The audience can now go home,
the play is over.

And yet I can't go. How can I possibly go, when I'm still
in such a daze as to how the play was actually played? As
to how it all happened. I've read it all, there's nothing else
in the record. But somehow or other I feel there is an act

missing. An act, not just a short scene. A whole act. I want
to talk to the players, meet the stars, try and find out
the details of the action.

But I don't want to talk to Jael! She's got a lot of talking
to do with Heber, and quite frankly I'd rather like to get
away before it starts. That will be a very interesting little
conversation piece, of that you may be sure, but it's got to
be another play altogether. And in any case I think I'm a
bit scared of Jael. That innocent-looking, "Here, my Lord,"
"Yes, my Lord," "Would this be just to your taste, my
Lord?" sort of cutie who floats prettily into the backyard
and the very next moment starts slamming a dirty big tent-
peg through a man's temple, and all the time humming a
saucy little aria from *Madame Butterfly*. I'm scared of ladies
like Jael, and you can quote me on that!

Nor Barak. He's just saying goodbye to Jael, "Thanks a
million, Jael," he's saying, "nice bit of wrist work. That
seven-pound sledge-hammer's a bit awkward for a little person like you, I'd have thought. I'll try and remember to send
round a neat little three-pound mash. Might come in handy.
There's still Jabin, you know. Keep your eye skinned."

No. Not Barak. I might as well ask myself the questions.
Barak's just as ordinary as I am.

But what about Deborah? Well, that's an idea. She's had
time to clean up after the battle. She was there, skirts and
all, but she should have had time to put on her face again
and tizzy her hair-do. Even write a short note to Lappidoth,
if she remembers where she put him! I think what a good
thing she didn't meet up with Sisera, she'd have just clobbered him over the head with a rock, imagine all the blood
and mayhem she would have stirred up.

But I'll take a chance with all that. I'll go up there and
find her if I can.

Deborah was there. Barak was there, too, he'd gone across
country by some short cut while I slowly followed the easier
tracks. I wasn't in a hurry, but I certainly did want to see
her.

She was there with Barak and a whole crowd of them.
It was night, and several large fires were still blazing, others
were just beginning to burn low. They had obviously been
celebrating, carousing and swapping tales of the day's heady
adventure. Deborah herself had been singing, she had
written it into a sort of poem and several groups were still
humming snatches from it as I moved among them.

Deborah, I said, you won't be able to sleep a wink tonight,
you're so excited. What a wonderful day. But I think it's
Ladies' Day. Your men were wonderful, I still can't get
over the way they just streamed down that hillside to meet
Sisera. But it's your day, really. Yours and Jael's. Tell me,
Deborah, what do you think of Jael? She's quite a tough
little puss, isn't she, with that wide-eyed innocence and that
butter-won't-melt-in-her-mouth sort of cuteness?

Deborah flipped through a stack of clay tablets on which
she had scribed her poem. She began to read, to sing. There
was music everywhere, excitement pulsed feverishly through
the whole encampment, even the crackling of the fires was
heady drama, there was a warmth no thermometer could
measure.

Perhaps it was part of this, perhaps all of this, that got
into me. Perhaps it was something of the Mahler Fifth that
I had heard only the night before, with the ominous pulse
of its funeral march, the complex weaving of the waltz in
the scherzo, the harsh brashness of the massed percussion in
the finale—some of this, all of this? I don't know. But
Deborah was reading, singing. Listen:

> *Blest above women be Jael,*
> *the wife of Heber the Kenite;*
> *blest above all women in the tents.*
> *He asked for water: she gave him milk,*
> *she offered him curds in a bowl fit for a chieftain.*

Her voice was gentle, low, all the roughness out of it, it
was the muted strings and reeds, reeds that were ever so
soft.

But now it rose—tenor sax, I said to myself, the harsh growl of the bassoon, just a hint of the power and the blare of the brass:

> *She stretched out her hand for the tent-peg,*
> *her right hand to hammer the weary.*

A moment's pause—that rest, that silent beat, that *tacet tutti* —and now it's all brass. Tuba, trombone, trumpet, the tympani and the percussion, a whole row of wild blowing horns——

> *With the hammer she struck Sisera, she crushed his*
> *   head;*
> *she struck and his brains ebbed out.*
> *At her feet he sank down, he fell, he lay;*
> *at her feet he sank down and fell.*
> *Where he sank down, there he fell, done to death.*

There was a fall in her voice, line by line, as she almost spat out those last three lines, the final "death" being just a wild, defiant gesture, not an audible sound at all. But the falling in her voice was matched by the rising roll of the side-drums and the clamour of the cymbals, their final staccato crash being lost in the mighty thunder of the bass-drum, with its slow-fading rumble seeming to go on, and on ... and on ..., carrying far away to the most distant mountain-top.

Jael, the wife of Heber, I was thinking to myself. That's what Deborah thinks of you, Jael. Cool, composed, clever little killer, Jael, the wife of Heber.

I thought I'd change the subject. Change the mood. Remember, I was standing there watching Jael spike that peg through Sisera's temple, and that was enough. I thought then that I had had more than enough—but this wild-eyed uninhibited re-enactment in the words and music of Deborah had me beaten. Yes, I thought, I'd change the subject. Take her into something lighter, into some soft, more feminine, more romantic mood.

Sure, Deborah, I said aloud, Jael's quite a girl. I just wonder if Heber knows yet what a charming little hostess his wife can be. It's Ladies' Day, and you can say that again! But Deborah, I wonder if there are any others in it with you? Any other women? I wonder if Sisera has left a wife? Or a mother?

My words were a question, really, not a statement. I wanted Deborah to answer me. But perhaps most of all I wanted to get her away from that sheer savagery of her account of Sisera's death. I just wanted that change of mood. I didn't want to risk meeting Deborah in a starring role in some heavy Wagnerian Tragedy.

Yes, I wanted that change of mood, but I was almost shattered by the change I got! For she got the message, she read the signal loud and clear, she answered me. But I was blithely thinking of the nineteenth-century romanticists, my thoughts were of background music by Chopin, Tchaikovsky, perhaps just Strauss. I was even quite happy to settle for a corny little piece of sweet, simple Dixieland.

But Deborah skipped over the whole lot. It wasn't even Beatle-land. It was shattering. She was jeering. She was mocking and taunting and scorning and teasing—and altogether and utterly hating, hating, hating!

The mother of Sisera peered through the lattice,
through the window she peered and shrilly cried,
"Why are his chariots so long coming?
Why is the clatter of his chariots so long delayed?"
The wisest of her princesses answered her,
yes, she found her own answer:
"They must be finding spoil, taking their shares,
a wench to each man, two wenches,
booty of dyed stuffs for Sisera,
booty of dyed stuffs,
dyed stuff, and striped, two lengths of striped stuff—
to grace the victor's neck."

She was singing from memory, I noticed. She had learned this part right off by heart, it was so obviously intense and bitter and real. That line about "a wench to each man, two wenches", almost made my cheeks blush, as I couldn't possibly miss the bitterness of the lust she was expressing. But the open taunt of Sisera's mother in that "two lengths of dyed stuff—to grace the victor's neck", was sheer hate-drenched murder.

I couldn't say anything. I couldn't applaud, I couldn't hiss—it wasn't a performance at all, it was an open glimpse into the very soul of Deborah herself.

But even as I stood silent, in a sudden full, rich, resonant contralto, she almost intoned:

So perish all thine enemies, O lord;
but let all who love thee be like the sun rising in strength.

Deborah stood still, the silence only accentuating the drama of those few short minutes. There was a look on her face rather like that on the face of the mother who gazes at her first born: surely, I thought, not on the face of the woman who has seen a whole army annihilated and its commander pinned to the earth with a tent-peg through his skull.

Phew, I am saying to myself. Deborah, how you hated Sisera. You hated his very guts, you surely did. Hmm, Deborah, I wonder why? I wonder whether you were yourself once one of those you sang about—"A wench for every man"? Were you once in Sisera's harem, even? Did you know him at such tragic first hand, know him perhaps in the foul intimacy of that sort of life? Or your sister perhaps? Or your daughter, your lovely teenage daughter?

But I don't say that aloud. I just pause a moment and say simply, Deborah, it's very hard for us humans to distinguish between hatred for evil-doers and hatred for the evil they do. Very hard. But you do at least remind us that evil is evil, and any man on earth who can't hate what is evil has no hope in Heaven of really loving what is good.

But I don't want to say more than that, Deborah. I don't
now even need to ask your opinion of the men who came to
the battle—I picked that up from a snatch or two of song
as I came through their lines. "Be proud at heart, you marshals of Israel", they were singing. And I nearly burst out
laughing! "Marshals of Israel", Deborah, and you never saw
a more disreputable looking bunch of ruffians. Bits of
Phoenician uniforms all over them, fitting only where they
actually touched, weapons they obviously didn't have a clue
in the world as to how to use, unwashed, blood-spattered—
"Marshals of Israel", Deborah. And yet you were right.
So right. This courage and this boldness and this day-long
fortitude is something no mere lineage, any more than a
mere décor, can supply. Only faith puts that into a man,
Deborah, and these ill-kempt scare-crows owe their prince-
liness to their relationship to God, not to man. But I don't
want to talk about them. Not now. Some day I'll take time
to stop and go right through your wonderful song of victory.

But Deborah, there is one thing I do want to know. I
saw these men set out from Mount Tabor. "Barak, today,"
you said. "Up! This day the Lord gives Sisera into your
hands. Already the Lord has gone out to battle before you."
Your exact words, Deborah. And I just shut my eyes.
I simply couldn't bear to watch the murderous, merciless
massacre. And when I opened my eyes at last, it was over.
There isn't a single bit of information given by the historian—merely a bald, unimaginative, tantalising comment:
"The Lord put Sisera to rout with all his chariots and his
army before Barak's onslaught." Just that. Deborah, please,
can you help me? This all sounds so absolutely nutty to me
that I almost wondered whether I was reading Hans Ander-
sen. Deborah, God is not a super-magician, waving some
magic wand and muttering heavenly Abracadabras and all
that circus jazz. God is the Creator, He is the Planner. "In
the beginning God created the heavens and the earth,"
Deborah. It was all there in the beginning. "In the beginning
was the Logos", Saint John interprets this. The Word, the
Divine Blue-Print, the detailed specification of the whole

cosmic purpose—and this great day of victory was on that
blue-print, Deborah. This fantastic day was planned then,
it's not a piece of off-the-cuff magic that God suddenly
thought up to get Himself and His people out of a jam.
God is not like that, He has never ever hinted that He is
the tiniest bit like that, even if lots of people do indeed
think that He is like that. No, Deborah, God is not like us
men—He is not made in man's image.

Can you help me in this? Does your wonderful epic poem
sing of this?

My first fleeting impression was that Deborah wouldn't
answer me. She's not the sort of dame who likes being
quizzed by a mere man, I was saying to myself. I'd better
be careful not to get her all upset.

But I needn't have bothered, for she just picked up two
of the clay moulds and handed them to me without demur.
Just a simple, "Here, these will help you, I'm sure." And
with her finger she traced out the characters on one of the
clay forms, as she chanted the words softly:

O Lord, at thy setting forth from Seir,
when thou camest marching out of the plains of Edom,
earth trembled, heaven quaked;
the clouds streamed down in torrents.
Mountains shook in fear before the Lord, the Lord of
  Sinai ...

She changed the two clay moulds in her hand, and turned to
the other:

Kings came, they fought;
then fought the kings of Canaan
at Taanach by the waters of Megiddo;
no plunder of silver did they take.
The stars fought from heaven
the stars in their courses fought against Sisera.
The Torrent of Kishon swept him away,
the Torrent barred his flight, the Torrent of Kishon;
  march on in might, my soul!

Deborah sang unaccompanied. But I didn't properly notice, even. Truth to tell, if she had had a hundred symphony orchestras and a score of massed bands, and anything else you cared to name playing with them, and all the hi-fi P.A. hook-ups you could wire together, it wouldn't have made a single decibel of difference. For I had my answer. I got the message. I saw how God did it. In the wonder of His patience and graciousness, God gave me a peep into His mind. Of all the hundreds of miracles recorded in His word, here, in one of the most incredible and bewildering of all, He takes me behind the scenes and lets me catch a glimmer of understanding. He actually shows me how He did it!

For now I don't go back three thousand years to see that day come into its dramatic climax—I go back three thousand million years to see it begin. For it was then, and it was there, in outmost space, that I see God working. Working for this one day, "the day the Lord gives Sisera into your hands!"

But it's not earth, it's not the solar system, it's not this galaxy at all, that I see. It's a star, a star that is exploding. God is exploding this star, as He has done so many countless others—but this one is for Sisera and Barak.

For Deborah is describing a thunderstorm. She is telling me that a great surging deluge flooded that little valley until it became a swirling water-covered morass.

Deborah, "the clouds streamed down in torrents", you said. You probably think, as everybody has thought for thousands of years, that "streaming" water is just the way it goes with clouds, that's all there is to it. But our meteorologists and astro-physicists are today beginning to understand and to grasp the wonder of the mechanisms involved. And there is no single wonder in it all that is as breath-taking as the wonder of a cloud itself. For clouds don't just "happen". Clouds don't simply turn up in the sky by some sort of party magic trick that leaves the audience gasping its applause while the conjurer starts repacking his little bag of tricks for tomorrow's show. No, of course not. Nothing like that. Clouds start with stars, stars that have exploded and have spread their "dust" into the limitless expanse of space. But this time some of that "dust" was planned to be caught up in the earth's atmosphere, and as each of these myriad particles becomes ionised by the sun's radiation, it forms the invisible nucleus on which water vapour condenses. The gas that was water is now the liquid that is water. For without the ionised particle on which to condense, the vapour will not become water. And it is here, away out here, almost at the end of nowhere-ness, it is on earth, that this time it is happening.

Deborah, it was Kishon, the little river Kishon trickling through that valley, that did it. As you say, "the Torrent of Kishon swept him away, the Torrent barred his flight, the Torrent of Kishon".

And of course! Of course! Those mighty Canaanite chariots. All that heavy, rich, expensive iron armament, all those massive, fearsome weapons—junk. Bogged down, fettered, doomed. The near-naked hills-men with their sticks and stones are now utterly and altogether on top. In swirling water and knee-deep mud, every amulet, shoulder-greave, breastplate and helmet becomes so much added menace. Every single ounce of ironmongery was an ounce nearer death. They were trapped, caught like rats, rats that were weighed down by every single thing that they had thought so valuable.

And God had known this, God had planned this, God had drawn it all up on that original, "in-the-beginning" blueprint. That unique concurrence of mechanisms, that final downpour that ended it all. For the precision of the planning matched the precision of the timing. "Barak, up! Today!" and I'm laughing out loud now. Barak—and I'm talking to Barak this time, I don't need to talk to Deborah any more—Barak, to think that I wondered what that "today" meant. Was it your wedding anniversary, somebody's birthday you'd forgotten, some tiny earth-sized trifle like that? Barak, what a cloth-headed dolt I have been. That "Barak, up! Today!" was the culmination of thousands of millions of years of planning and precise, detailed manipulation of the essential hardware of the whole universe. Barak, just how dumb can I be?

And I burst into a great guffaw of laughter, laughing now at my own feeble human littleness, laughing in exultant delight at catching just this tiny glimpse of the real greatness of God.

And even as I laugh, even as I slap my thigh in wonderment, something almost cuts my breath in my throat. A horrible, ice-cold dread, nearly stops me breathing altogether. There are beads of perspiration forming on my forehead, it's hard to keep writing because of a wretched tremor that clutches my hand.

For I remember something else. Something else about that "Barak, up! Today!" I remember clearly, ever so clearly, something else I said then. I said that "if God had told me to do anything as crazy as that I'd be arguing it out with Him still. And I'd certainly spend the whole of that day asking just why it should be today and not tomorrow."

Yes, arguing, with my three pounds of brain, as to why it should be today and not tomorrow. Arguing: and now I see that the "today" of God is the fulfilment of the thousands of millions of years that constitutes all time. The event of today is the accomplishment of all the machinery that we call space and matter.

Yes, again. For that "today" was something that would never happen again. Never. That little plain of Megiddo, that Jezreel valley into which Barak went charging so precipitously at God's call of "today", has seen more fighting, has drunk in more human blood, than perhaps any other equal sized piece of land on all this earth's surface. The history of the human race has time and again been determined on that very same battlefield. But Torrent Kishon, the tiny river that became the mighty rushing Torrent, is unique. Utterly unique. That didn't happen any old day in the week. That flood wasn't the thing the farmers had to look out for every spring. You wouldn't hear about it even in the reminiscences of the oldest inhabitants down in the local pub. Why, you won't even find a single reference to a

flood like that in the literature. That flash-flood from that
cloud-burst was a once-in-a-history-book event!

For the simple truth is that God planned every second of
time as He planned every centimetre of space as He planned
every gramme of matter. That "today" of God is unique
because God insists that every day is unique. No wonder my
head is in my hands and my whole being is in such bitter
confusion. Fancy arguing all the first day as to why it should
be today and not tomorrow ...

Do you wonder why this story so stirs me, speaks so
clearly and directly to me?

For it is not Deborah's story, after all. It's not her name
that is recorded in that wonderful Honours Roll, it's Barak's.
Deborah might have been the judge, she may well have been
the prophetess, she is perhaps a dozen other things you could
think of. But you don't find her name listed in that famous
eleventh chapter of the Epistle to the Hebrews. And it's not
Jael's story, even though Deborah said all the glory would
go to a woman. That's just her opinion, I'd say, because I
don't call that glory at all. Not in a woman. Certainly not
in my woman. I like the sort of "glory" Saint Paul writes
about in a woman—the glory that shows itself in being "loving
wives and mothers, temperate, chaste, and kind, busy at
home ..."—that cute little trick with tent-pegs is something
I don't dig at all, however brave and resourceful she may
have been with it. No, no, of course it's not Jael's story.

It's altogether God's story. And yet it's still Barak's story.
That's what makes it so compelling, that's what really grips
me by the heart. For Barak is the simple, ordinary, uncomplicated, inconspicuous man God just landed with the job.
A mere anybody, Barak is—I said "I might as well ask myself
the questions. Barak's just as ordinary as I am."

Yes, Barak's as ordinary as I am ordinary or any other
man is ordinary. It is God who makes him so different. It's
because he is one of God's men, he's one of the men of
faith, that his name is in that altogether illustrious Honours
Roll.

And that's the real answer to the real question: the question of meaning and of purpose and of reality. The meaning of life is as clear as the goal of life—God. Not told in rhetoric and philosophy and debate—told in the life and the daily tasks that constitute the story of any man at all. It's not a matter of a religion, it's entirely a matter of a relationship. It's not the problem of the naked ape seeking a solution to his loneliness and his feeling of guilt and his sense of despair. No. Nothing like that. It's just a matter of finding out what God wants, and doing it.

GIDEON

To the average Aussie, who lives in a city but who goes for a four or five hundred mile drive in his car almost any weekend, one of the problems in understanding the Old Testament is the geography of Palestine.

For in the first place it is so tiny. Such a cramped up, miniature affair altogether, that when he reads of the Hittites, the Perizzites, the Jebusites and what-not other-ites, he loses all good perspective. In fact, just commuting to work every day is likely to take him much further than the territory that any dozen of these -ites may contain. And the weekend jaunt, down to the snow-country, up to the northern beaches, along the south coast, west over the mountains—any one of a score of such trips—would more than cover the whole of Palestine several times over. In one Army Hospital in which I was working during the war, one of the other M.O.s came from a cattle ranch in Northern Queensland, where his father owned ten thousand square miles of country. Six and a half million acres. You could put the whole of Palestine down in their backyard. Of course this is the exception, the average Aussie owns merely a pocket-handkerchief piece of monotonous suburbia, but he does also own a six-cylinder, six-seater motor car, and the whole vastness of his country tends to rub off on to his thinking. And that makes the geography of Palestine a bit of a puzzle to him. That is one problem.

And the other is the fact that the country runs down hill. In every other country in the world, as you travel in from the coast you travel up hill; or, at the least, you find yourself on plains or tablelands. But in Palestine it's different. After a very few miles, twenty or thirty at the most, the land gradient starts to slope downwards, and bless your soul, in almost no time at all you find yourself down below sea-level. The deep Jordan–Dead Sea valley is away down underground, if you get the idea I am trying to convey. So that many of the rivers are flowing backwards, really, flowing away from the sea, flowing into the central land mass. Now we do have the same thing in Australia, of course, with our vast inland seas; but that is in the "Dead Heart" as we call it, the desert land of Central Australia, and that is so far from anywhere that it simply doesn't matter.

But in Palestine it's very different. The low-lying, below-sea-level Jordan is still very important countryside in their economy: what goes on there is of the utmost significance. While east of the Jordan, on the inland side, the hills rise precipitously again, giving the whole land an almost fenced-off limitation, with merely an occasional *wadi* or mountain pass leading out through the tableland to the desert in the east.

All so precipitous, so tiny, so back-to-front. And altogether so locked in by the Mediterranean on the west and the hills and desert on the east and south, with this unique Jordan Valley cleft, so deeply carved into the earth's surface, right in the middle.

Now all this is important, highly important, to a proper understanding of the story of Gideon.

For Gideon lived near the northern limit of the Jordan, on the hills above the Sea of Galilee. And across the Jordan was another valley which broke through the eastern mountain ranges into the Arabian Desert itself. Gideon's home was only about twenty miles from where Barak lived. But twenty miles that might just as well have been two hundred. For Barak looked down on the valley of Megiddo, you remember, with the little Kishon river trickling westwards to the Mediterranean. While Gideon looked down on to a valley that carried the streams and creeks eastwards to the Jordan. And on the other side of the Jordan was this wide, low-level mountain pass that gave almost direct access to the desert further east still.

And this was the bit of geography that brought Gideon into history; this is what gives us one of the most fabulous stories ever recorded.

For through this mountain pass from the desert had streamed the Bedouin. For the first time in human history the desert people had domesticated the camel, the problem of transport across the endless sands was now solved, the "ship of the desert" was now a new factor in the story of man's aggression and survival in this world.

But Gideon wasn't involved in the domestication of camels and their training as desert transport. He was concerned with the problem of protection from the camel owners, the marauding Arabs who now came padding in through the mountain passes on their raiding missions. And Gideon felt, as his people felt, the utterly hopeless nature of their problem. For the desert raiders could come loping in over the sands in sudden silence out of literally nowhere, make a lightning raid, and then disappear into smoke before anyone could do much more than shout a warning.

And the more you think over this problem the more hopeless you must see it to be. For the two obvious answers are equally useless. One answer is to move further up into the mountains. Get up into the steeper hillsides where the big lumbering camels aren't much good, and thus use the terrain itself as a simple protection. And this was what the people actually did. They moved higher and higher up from the reach of the desert people until they were literally living in the dens and caves and mountain strongholds. They did just that. But the problem with that is the simple fact that you then starve to death. Safe from the marauding Arabs, but those craggy hills don't grow enough food to keep body and soul together. Death by starvation is the price of that system.

The other obvious solution is to gather a strong standing army and police the mountain passes into the desert. But again, standing armies need feeding and maintaining, and unless you start off with plenty of food and equipment then you still all starve to death making it work. They didn't even try that one!

And if you are naïve enough to suggest just going out and attacking the Arabs when they did turn up *en masse*, then think again. You can't do it. It's like sending the army out to attack the navy. All they need to do is up anchor and sail over the horizon and then where are you? Have they gone north? Have they gone south? Have they gone anywhere at all, or are they riding at sea-anchor just out of sight from land, waiting till you have all gone home, then to come pouncing in again just where you last saw them? You simply can't do it. Out in those desert dunes every yard becomes a mile, and any poor fool who goes charging into that burning waste will finish up a pile of sun-bleached bones on the windswept expanse of sand.

It was a bleak enough outlook indeed. And Gideon was a young man in that wretched little district. And the people tried every trick they knew, to defeat and thwart the Arabs, and all to no avail. They were still hungry, unsettled and in danger.

Until at last they began to cry to God for help. And God sent a prophet among them to give them His answer.

Now if you think of prophets in the Bible as being long-haired recluses who lived in huge mountain monasteries and spent their days praying in between meals of bread and water and only ever spoke in out-of-date Elizabethan English in jargon ordinary people never used or understood—then you haven't been reading your Bible at all. You got your ideas from fairy books or stained-glass windows, whichever are the more misleading.

Prophets are men of affairs. They are workers, tradesmen, farmers, statesmen. They are as practical as today's lunch or tomorrow's clean shirt.

And this one was no exception. As he came through the place and learned the complaint and lament of the people, he listened carefully and heard them out. But he wasn't one bit deceived. They were only complaining, they weren't really praying. "Listen," he said, "you seem to have forgotten something. You have forgotten just who you are and how you got here. You were slaves, don't you remember? Slaves in Egypt. That's what you were. And you'd still be there if God hadn't rescued you. He brought you out of Egypt and slavery. And He told you clearly and directly that He was

to be your only God. You were to get completely away
from worshipping the gods and religions of the indigenous
people here where He brought you. You were to forget these
other gods, and worship Him only. Now! Look there behind
you. You just look around. You see what has happened?
You simply haven't obeyed Him, and no wonder you are in
this mess!"

And he turned on his heel and walked off. Shades of
Dale Carnegie and how *not* to win friends and influence
people!

And the people couldn't answer him, because there, smack
in the middle of the village square, right under their noses,
were the Baal and Asherah of the religions of the people
they had tangled with.

It was all very depressing, and nobody seemed to have an
answer. And one who certainly had no answer to the prophet
was Gideon. He had no answer because he wasn't even there
when all this was going on. Gideon was not the sort of man
who spent a lot of his time on ritual ceremonies and support of the effete establishment. Gideon was pretty tired of
it all and he was more interested in food.

Gideon's food-interest showed in a trick he had developed
to hoodwink the Arabs. He grew his bit of grain, and then
threshed and ground it in the wine-press. And when attacked
from the desert he could hope to escape discovery by this
simple subterfuge.

So Gideon was working away heading out his grain when
a man strolled up. The man was actually a messenger to him
from God; and I have no doubt at all that this was the
prophet himself, only too glad to be getting away after his
highly unfruitful meeting in the village; and if that is my
idea as to who the man was—and it is, you are quite entitled
to yours—it was most assuredly something Gideon did not
know. But whether or not it was the prophet is beside the
point—there may just possibly have been two such men
touring those outback parts of Manasseh on the same day,
and that would be most remarkable indeed, and you can
say that again! It was still fairly early morning, and Gideon

was already hard at it. The visitor didn't ask Gideon why he had been absent from the big village-meeting that morning—he did what any normal man of affairs does when he sees somebody working—he sat down to watch. There was a big oak tree there to shade them both from the heat, and that's how it was: Gideon toiling away at his grinding and the messenger sitting wiping his brow after a rather short but fiery sermon.

A nice enough little rustic scene if ever you like. The casual "Good morning" and "Nice day" and "Like a swig from my water-bottle? Nice and cool you'll find it." "Thanks. Don't mind if I do. I'm pretty dry I admit." You know how it goes, all very rural and countrified and ordinary.

Gideon had stopped to take a breather and was just mopping his wet forehead when the other man looked hard at him and said, "Gideon, you're quite a fellow. You've got all the guts in the world, haven't you? God must certainly be with you."

Gideon's answer was as quick and pat as anything in Bernard Shaw. "Sir," he flashed back, "I don't get the logic of that. If God is with us, then why are we in all this mess? I know how the usual line of argument goes. Some of our tribal elders talk like this. The 'Did not the Lord bring us up out of Egypt?' sort of spiel; but I'm sure I'm not impressed. If God did really do all that, then He's slipped somewhere! We might have been rescued from the Egyptians, but we're certainly in the clutches of the Arabs now. No, I'm not impressed."

The visitor pursed his lips, not with dismay or annoyance, but with obvious pleasure and approval! "Gideon!" he exclaimed, "that's splendid! Just splendid!"

He rose from where he had been squatting on a large root of the old oak, and came over to put his hand on Gideon's shoulder. "The very man! Gideon, you have just what it takes. I want you to use this splendid strength and courage to deliver your people of Israel from the desert invaders. It's the very job for you, and I'm happy to put it officially into your most capable hands."

Gideon quietly raised his left hand and slowly and very deliberately lifted the other man's hand from his right shoulder where it was still resting. There was a studied politeness in his voice that fully matched the icy coolness in his words. "Sir, your logic again eludes me. I, deliver Israel? I must remind you, sir, that I belong to the humblest clan in all my tribe of Manasseh, and I am actually the youngest member in my family. Sir, what you suggest is simply not possible."

I don't even know the man's name, let alone his background and his qualifications. But this man was speaking as the messenger of God. "Gideon," he said firmly, warmly, enough sympathy to keep contact, yet enough sternness to demand respect, "you are not the one to say that. It's not a matter of your opinion. It must be mine. And in my opinion you are in fact the right man, and it is a matter of my appointing you to the task, not of your deciding on your own fitness for the task. Gideon, I speak with the Voice of God: I say you are in fact the man of choice, you have my full confidence. And I assure you that you will absolutely trounce those Bedouin people, you'll beat the pants off them!"

It was strong, clear, incisive, direct. And it drew in Gideon the response you might expect. Gideon was a man of lightning mind, great imagination, keen sense of drama and timing.

"All right, sir! If all you say about me is what you genuinely think, then I'll take your word for it, that you do honestly and sincerely mean what you say. But just because *you* believe it—that doesn't mean a thing to me. I can't accept it just because you do, no matter how convinced you happen to be. Sir, I'd need far better evidence than that. No, sir, it's up to you to prove it—prove that I should lead the attack on the Arabs."

Gideon was not being difficult, there was no truculent tantrum building up—but he certainly meant it.

And Gideon bowed slightly, turned on his heel, and went back to his grinding.

And his visitor went back to his seat on the root of the

huge oak and went back to his watching, legs crossed comfortably, shoulders resting against the enormous trunk, quite unruffled, all the time in the world.

It was Gideon who made the next move. The man who really knows the Voice of God is not going to be making panic moves just because a Gideon is cautious. No, he can relax, God knows what He is doing.

So that it was Gideon who made the next move. The sun was now directly overhead, it was close to noon, and a clever, quick-thinking mind like his could find the answers without a kindergarten teacher making him spell out each letter in every word. "Sir," he said after this almost age-long silence, "if you could really prove to me that what you say is true, then I'll do it. I don't really doubt you. I certainly don't really doubt God, but it's myself I'm not sure about. Sir, if it's not asking too much altogether, then a clear, unmistakable sign would be all I'd need. Now, sir, I'll go and get some food—I'll prepare it carefully as an offering. I'll be right back. Will you please wait here?"

Now when we read this tale in the Bible, our western minds often find it hard to realise just what is really happening. "So Gideon went in, prepared a kid and made an ephah of flour into unleavened cakes. He put the meat in a basket, poured the broth into a pot and brought it out to him under the terebinth."

That's what we read. Just a simple little matter, Gideon buzzed off for a couple of minutes to knock up the makings of a bit of a decent snack. Yes, we think, quite generous—we'd probably offer the chap a cool drink, care for some coffee? Black or white? Could you stay for lunch, sir? A quick dip in the fridge, whip up some girdle cakes on the frypan or some savoury waffles on the new automatic iron. Sure, sir, please make yourself comfortable, here is the latest *Punch*. Have you seen this morning's paper? I won't be more than a few minutes.

Now I admit that I have almost perfected the three-minute luncheon. And the hurried meal is just a part of our modern high-velocity world. But Gideon's book of etiquette had no doubt told him that the preparing and the eating of a meal was a matter of hours. Travellers tell me that the same customs still hold in the Middle East even today. So that it was the very best party manners which guided Gideon as he went off to catch a kid, kill it, dress it, mix the batter and concoct the "broth", whatever that is. But it still all sounds to me like at least a couple of hours hard work. I don't know, I'm not a chef, I don't even know if any of it was cooked or left to be baked later. But I think the "broth" must have been the sort of "stock-pot" goo that many country folk keep simmering away on their kitchen stoves almost year in, year out. Sure, it still sounds like a long time. And the visitor had skimmed through *Punch* and glanced over the headlines in the paper, and was browsing through the classified ads before Gideon came back with it all prepared. Basket in one hand, and in the basket was the dressed, jointed, kid. In his other hand the stock-pot with the "broth" bubbling thick steamy heat. And the "cakes", or damper, or batter—call it the name most appropriate—probably on top of the meat in the basket.

But if it all took two minutes or two hours, the messenger had waited on, and now he took over the rest of the show. He knew what to do.

"Splendid, Gideon. The meat first, please. Put it on this rock. That's it, right there. And the cakes, now, Gideon, beside the meat—right, that's the way exactly. Now take the broth, and pour some of it over them all. Steady ... slowly ... Yes, a little more now ... Good. Now stand back."

I know what some of you are probably thinking. All this Gideon-meets-padre stuff is jolly good show, there ought to be more of it—our world's a bit weak in its religion, too—but it's not exactly high, heady drama. Gideon dashing off to kill the kid and bring back the meal is very like afternoon tea at the vicarage, and without Agatha Christie around with her Hercule Poirot to dig up a murder or two it's just so plain dull that it's thoroughly boring. Not like Ehud—the moment we first saw him he had a dagger strapped to his thigh, remember? And Sisera started off the tale of Barak for us, and Sisera had nine hundred iron chariots. Pretty crummy little horse-drawn machines, of course, but there'd be nothing more exciting in the world for nearly three thousand years, and at least there's a bit of real action every time we remember those chariots. But not this Gideon character. A rather trite bit of metaphysical discussion and coffee with the preacher—not exactly sparkling, is it? Even if the parson bloke had been a bishop, that doesn't lift the action much—bishops in Australia don't even make page five in our dailies unless they drop some awful brick or come out with something particularly crazy. Well, thanks for the story, I'll leave you with Gideon and his clerical companion while they go on discussing the state of the nation and I'll get back to the sporting pages—I'm tipping we'll have two slow bowlers in the team for England next winter and I must see what the newspaper boys are saying. So long—I'll leave you eating the lunch with them ...

Oh no, you don't! Not a bit. That meal wasn't eaten at all. For the dull, slow start of the story became instant action, as literally in a sudden blaze of flame the whole story goes up.

I don't know how it happened. I can guess, and you can guess if you like. My guess is that it was the thick fat in the "broth". As I said, I'm not a chef, I have the happy good fortune to be married to a superb little housekeeper, real *cordon bleu* class, and I never have to give a thought in the world as to how the mystic processes of a kitchen work their magic. No, I'm lucky and I know it. But just as Gideon poured the last of that heavily fatted broth over the meat and the cakes, the prophet leaned over with the tip of his staff and pouff!, the whole thing·burst into leaping flames.

Now you see what I mean. The action has started, and started well and truly. For as Gideon blinked his eyes and stepped back, the messenger vanished!

Terrific! Real Tivoli stuff. Fine act. Clever build-up, all so very quiet and chatty, the audience just beginning to

shuffle its feet and hope it won't be long, it's time the chorus
came back; witch-doctors and those quaint characters usually
turn up with some pretty exciting magic, but this chap is
obviously borrowed from the reserve grade team, and it's
not really so—Whooff! Boy, that was a good act! I was
barely watching. I must come back again some other night
and see it again—it's a winner. That wasn't petrol or butane
he was using. I know *that*, at any rate. No petrol or butane
in his time, I remember. But of course the hot fat was pretty
nearly volatile, kitchens are always catching alight like that,
it's the commonest household fire accident. By George,
though, I wonder was that wand electrostatically non-con-
ducting? Was this a multi-thousand voltage discharge from
rubbing against his cloak? No nylon petticoats for operating
theatre staff, I remember, because of sparking risks with
ether or cyclo. Yes, but what about the tip of the wand—
was it metal-tipped? Was this a contact potential, just
hundreds of years before Galvani and Volta? Hey, Gideon,
I call out excitedly, did you see what happened? Are you all
right? I hope you didn't get too much smoke in your eyes.
But tell me, did you get a chance to see how he did it? You
were quite close. You'd make a whole packet of dough playing that round the camp-fires at night as a vaudeville act.
Tell me, Gideon, what do you know?

But Gideon isn't answering me. Gideon's face is still
buried in his hands. But it's not smoke, it's not a sore eye
and a smarting conjunctiva that makes him hold his face to
the ground.

No. Gideon is bowed in prayer, not in pain. It's not a
sore eye, it's a broken heart. For he has seen the messenger
of God, and seen him face to face. And much more poignantly, the young man knows that he has really seen God,
he has seen God face to face.

I stand awkwardly, not knowing now quite what to say.
For I have seen only a side-show act, a bit of party magic.
But Gideon has seen only God at work, he has seen only
miracle. And the bowed head and laboured breathing show
his despair, not his excitement. God has met him, and his

life is forfeit. He is to die ...

And even as I stand there, Gideon rises. His hands drop from his face, his head is now held high, he is light of step and bright of eye. It's a new Gideon altogether!

For with the fast thinking that we will come to find so remarkable in all his future, Gideon has got his answer: God met him, God consumed the meal in the flames that are still leaping from the boiling fat—but God did not consume him. God has accepted him. God has surely accepted him!

Yes! Gideon is now accepted, God is with him, he and God are at peace.

"So Gideon built an altar there to the Lord and named it 'The Lord is peace'."

You guessed it correctly. A man like Gideon, teamed up with God, at peace with God, is not going to sit around for goodness knows how long and just wait for something to happen. Gideon now knows what it feels like to be at peace with God, and the sheer compulsion of that immense freedom is now his guide.

The idea came to him that night, that very first night.

He waited until the following night to put it into action, and that was not being cowardly or timorous or lily-livered. No, that was just being sensible. For what he was going to do was dynamite, and a fast-thinking, imaginative man like Gideon must give proper heed to prudence and propriety. Of course, mere prudence and propriety don't control him any longer, God controls him; but they must certainly guide him. Gideon is not Barak, good, simple, solid, yokel Barak who doesn't ask a single question. Not a bit. Gideon must think, he must use the alert, sharp brain that is within his skull, the brain that is now in the control of God.

So Gideon waited till night. And while his local tribesmen slept the night through, he did his stuff.

He took ten trusted workmen, and away they went. They ripped up the altar that Gideon's father had built for the worship of the Baal, the heathen deity of the local nation, chopped up the Asherah, the sacred wooden pillar, or totem-pole, that stood beside the Baal, and built a traditional Israelite altar of sacrifice. And the sacrificial animal was none other than dad's yearling bull, his number two beast.

Oh boy. Did that start a brawl? When the locals crept out of bed the next morning and strolled up to the "grove" where they did their religious routine, the place was a shambles. The Baal altar a heap of ruins, the Asherah chopped to matchwood and the yearling bull laid out ready to be cooked!

No need to call in Scotland Yard. Sherlock Holmes can forget this case. Gideon and his ten men working like beavers all night leave a trail about a mile wide.

"Hey, Joash. It's your youngest brat, Gideon. He's the wrecker." "Yes, he's done this. He'll get what's coming to him!" "Yes, Joash, bring him out, right now, the ——, and we'll settle with him."

And there is Joash, old father Joash, the fellow who actually made the Baal and the Asherah, coming to the front door to hear all the dreadful things his brat of a youngest son had done, to hear how his Baal had been pulverised, its totem a mere heap of kindling wood, and his yearling bull, the bull he had been reckoning as his number one replacement beast—mincemeat. If ever a son was due for the wigging of a lifetime, Gideon had drawn the unlucky number.

I don't know how you see Joash, but if I were casting the story of Gideon for a Hollywood production I'd get a Stanley Holloway type of player. I see him as a Yorkshireman. The only genuine Yorkshireman in the Bible. I'd try and make him look about five feet five inches tall, chest forty-eight, listening to the tale of general desolation and mayhem. I'd get him standing at the door with his big boots about twenty inches apart, coat thrown back from ample belly, thumbs hooked in the armpits of his waistcoat with a heavy gold chain bespangling his mid-line, multiple chins resting firmly on his chest—altogether a most redoubtable old gentleman!

And I'd cast him like this because Joash was Joash. I can't see anybody less than a Yorkshireman possessing the

speed and acuity of perception together with the dour
stolidity to stand there and hurl it all back in their teeth.
Yes, back in the very teeth of the townsfolk. For hard-headed
and dour and stolid and everything else that only a Joash
(or another Yorkshireman) can be, with lightning speed the
old boy saw the truth. And there was a flash in his eye and
a taunt in his tone that whipped those villagers more sharply
than any lash or stick could ever achieve.

But whether you choose to translate his words into the
dialectal Yorkshire idiom, or try and imagine it in its original
Hebrew, or just take it in the words of modern English,
Joash had his reply ready in a trice. And he had it clear.
Crystal clear. Like this: "But as they crowded around him
Joash retorted, 'Are you pleading Baal's cause then? Do
you think that it is for you to save him? Whoever pleads
his cause shall be put to death at dawn. If Baal is a god
and someone has torn down his altar, let him take up his
own cause.'" And inside the house, jumping up and down
in sheer excitement, is Gideon, hearing it all. And as the
shame-faced locals crept back to work, all the fire knocked
clean out of them, Gideon now knew. He had got his answer.
He had checked it out with God, and God had given him the
all-clear.

For this was what Gideon had been doing as he hacked
away at the Baal and the Asherah that night. Gideon had
been running a simple test; he had, as it were, been taking
a sample for analysis. And the report had come back favour-
able. Gideon wasn't checking out on God. That is never
Gideon, any more than it is ever any other man of faith.
Gideon had been checking out on himself. For already he
had the germ of an idea; but it was an idea that had to be
approved by God. And this Baal-wrecking incident was
another idea again, in which he had really been asking God
to guide him—the green light with dad and the bull and the
Baal would tell him that he could expect the green light for
this other, even more hazardous scheme . . .

In through the mountain passes and over the Jordan

crossings streamed the Bedouin hosts, the whole valley black with them and their camels.

And Gideon got the message. He got it clear, he got it straight. God was now calling him to tackle the Arabs. That was the challenge. That was the challenge Gideon accepted. Out into all the surrounding countryside, into all his Israelite tribes, went the runners. The call was for volunteers to come and fight.

His own villagers, the locals who had seen what he did to his dad's Baal, were the first to line up. And then in began to stream the others. Hundreds of them, thousands of them.

There they were, 32,000 finally, looking down the hill-slopes at the Arab encampment. "Ha!" you say, "this is more like it. No more of this Barak and his puny troops dashing half-naked and helpless down under the very hooves of the chariot horses. This is much more even, now we will see a real test of strength."

Not so fast, though. That Arab encampment was vast. It filled the whole of the plains for miles. Right back to the very Jordan crossing. Over 135,000 fighting men alone, in that invasion force, perhaps even many more than that still.

Hmmm ... 135,000 plus is a lot of troops, then as now. Mountbatten took 120,000 into Singapore with him in his task force at the end of the war, and the hospital I then belonged to was on board one of those troopships in that vast flotilla. A lot of ships, a lot of men. And Gideon was looking down on many more still.

And being Gideon, alert, clear-thinking Gideon, he had to rethink it all. For he had 32,000; and the Arabs had about five times as many: now what to do? Check with God, that's what he decided to do.

"God," he prayed, "I just want simple redirection. Just to be sure that I am doing what You really want me to do, and not just following my own ideas. Now God, I have a very straightforward test. I'm putting a fleece out tonight on the ground we use for a threshing floor. If the fleece is wet with dew in the morning, and at the same time all the ground around it is dry, then I'll have my answer. Then

I'll know that You will deliver Your people under my leadership, as I already think You have told me."

And sure enough, next morning the ground was dry and the fleece was wringing wet. Gideon squeezed a whole bowlful of water out of it.

That's Gideon. That's what he's like. His sort of brain. In fact, even more like that still. It would be two and a half thousand years before the first men of science began to ask the questions that would challenge and change every statement of natural philosophy that the world had previously known; but Gideon had the type of mind that makes a good scientist. He questioned his answer.

"Oh, God," he prayed again, "please forgive me, and don't get absolutely mad with me. But I'm still not really sure. Could You reverse the mechanism? Make the fleece bone-dry, with all the ground wet with dew? If You do that, I have no more questions to ask."

Terrific! Superb! Gideon wasn't prevaricating. He wasn't wavering, doubting, terrified, overawed, trying to back out, or anything like it. He wasn't a bit scared by the 135,000 Arabs. Not for a moment. The God who could flash flames from the tip of the staff in a visiting messenger's hand could easily enough account for any number of Arabs the desert could spew up. The God who could get under the skin of his stocky, stuck-in-the-mud, old dad Joash so deeply as to get the old man all anti-Baal-defence—that God would have no trouble at all with Arabs. No, Gideon had no doubts at all about God. His mind was too clear, his intelligence too great, to have to go over that again and again. His doubt was not in God, it was in himself.

Out went the fleece again, this time to be bone-dry in the middle of the wet, dewy threshing floor.

Now Gideon knew, and knew for utter certainty. One wet fleece on dry ground could just possibly be accident, coincidence. But not one wet fleece on dry ground *plus* one dry fleece on wet ground.

Gideon was in business. God had really called him, God was in fact asking him to see it through. There he was, 32,000 men; and enough Arabs to go round five apiece. Gideon, it's over to you.

Gideon looked at them. He looked at his men, he looked at the Arabs, he looked back at his men—and he had his answer.

"Men. Attention! I want you to listen carefully. You see all those Arabs down there—myriads of them. There are 32,000 of us here. Long odds against us. Now I want to make this quite clear: if any of you would like to call it a day and nip back home, now's your opportunity. I don't want anybody with me who is not thoroughly happy with his chances. Don't be embarrassed, no mock heroics. If you don't stomach it, if you feel the least bit squeamish about it, then off you go. Only stay if you really have a heart for it."

And off they streamed. First a trickle, then a good flow, finally a cascade; 22,000 of them walked off. Two-thirds. Ten thousand remaining. And still 135,000 fully-armed Arab fighting men, plus the rest of their entourage.

Ten thousand. Gideon looked at them, looked at the Arabs again, looked back at his men, and got his next answer.

"Men. Attention! It's time to be on the march. Now our first move will be down to the spring for a good long drink and then we're on our way. In double column, march."

Gideon had his plan. He knew what to look for, and he found it. As the men came to the water point, he stood and watched as they drank. Some of them (most of them) stopped at the water and knelt down to get a drink. These he directed to his left. The others (the few) just lapped the water, scooped up in cupped hands, face-first like a dog. These he formed up in a small company on his right. They were only three hundred strong.

"Men. Attention! You men over on my left, I want you to go home. Be ready to come when I call you, but I don't want you now. Quick march!"

And off went the army! Two-thirds had gone the day before, now he had only three hundred left.

"OK men. Gather round me and pay close attention. This is our plan of attack ..."

Hmmm, I'm saying to myself. What-ho for Barak and his ten thousand again. This is even worse! The thunderstorm that God had prepared with all the resources of His Cosmos for just that occasion was certainly enough to fill all men with awe and wonder. But something far bigger is needed this time. Something about the size of an H-bomb. What say a really king-sized meteor? Perhaps a ghastly epidemic of something. Something like smallpox, plague, cholera, epidemic pneumonia 'flu. Malaria might do it, if God can get the mossies buzzing thickly enough. But any infection toxic enough to decimate the Arab encampment would need to be highly virulent and it would make a pretty risky occupation area for the petty three hundred Israelite attackers. Yes, I wonder if God really knows this answer?

And Gideon is wondering, too. Not wondering about God, as I am, wondering about himself, still.

This time his answer is different. "Purah, here a moment." Purah is his batman, his personal orderly. "Purah, what say you and I go down into the Arab camp tonight and simply give it a little look over? It's just a hunch I have. Like to be in on it?"

And down they sneak. They are all Semites, really, and disguise is no problem. Getting past the sentries is a pushover. In fact it is doubtful whether the Arabs have bothered to post sentries in more than token strength, the very idea of attack is almost laughable. So that in the dark, more still in the very enormity and the vastness of the encampment, two men can come and go and never be detected. There they are, right inside. All around them, myriads of men and flocks and camels.

Oh, I say to myself again, this is incredible. Just what on earth is God going to do? What in heaven can He do? Gideon and his three hundred men could come in here with machine-guns and field artillery and bazookas and just anything you could name, and all they would do is shoot down a few odd thousands and pile up a heap of horses and camels before it's over. Down they'd go in an avalanche of flesh. Oh, God, I don't want to be irreverent, but I just feel that You'll need to think up something pretty fantastic this time. I'm awfully bothered. I'll go and stay with Gideon and Purah, in case they get into trouble; but please, God, keep thinking. It looks absolutely hopeless to me.

Gideon and Purah are stopping. There they are, just outside the faint glow of the weak beam of light coming through an open tent flap. Inside the tent there are voices. Arab voices. "Listen, you fellows." It's an Arab speaking. "Hey, listen to me, you coves. I'm worried. I had a dream last night and I dreamed I saw a little barley loaf come tumbling into our camp and it hit this tent such a wallop that it wrecked the thing absolutely. Knocked it head over turtle, and there it was, right flat on the ground."

I can hear just the faintest hiss of indrawn breath from Gideon, who is half-crouching beside me, his head absolutely motionless and one ear cocked slightly forward in excitement.

"Do you know what I think that means?" The Arab's tent-mate is now speaking. "I think that means Gideon. This is the attack of Gideon, the son of Joash, one of the Israelites. It means God has given all the Bedouin army into his hand! My, I'm scared!"

I stand for a moment in sheer astonishment. This crazy Arab dreamer and his crazier interpreter are surely psycho! I guess I know what it means, I say to myself. These fellows probably saw the 32,000 men that Gideon had collected up, and they saw them disappear, and they are wondering what has happened to them. Here they are, all goose-pimply and in a panic, wondering if they are on a flanking movement or something, ready to pounce in from some unexpected quarter! Little do they know! Those 32,000 are all nicely tucked up under the blankets at home with mum and the kids, and the very idea of any harm arising from them is just too fancy for words.

And the guffaw that rises within me is cut short as I see

that Gideon and Purah have gone—there they are, streaking up the shadowy hillside, back to their tiny little band of three hundred men. And I'm as bewildered as I'm puffed, for as I come panting up with them, Gideon has already got them mobilised. They're on the way! They're going to attack the Arab army!

Yes, they're marching, and not even a single field piece among them. Not even a Bren gun. And I blink my eyes and look again, staring terribly hard now through the night shadows, for there's not even a bow and arrow! They've got a bit of a dagger tucked into their girdles, but they're really completely unarmed. And look—they've got a big earthenware water-pot held awkwardly in one hand; and it looks like a ram's horn, that high-pitched unmusical "trumpet" they love to blow on, hanging from a cord round their necks. But that's all. Here, Gideon, wait a moment ...

But Gideon has gone, streaking silently, purposefully, up over the high ground overlooking the invading army.

Oh, God, I am saying, this is the absolute dizzy limit. Ehud and Eglon I can understand, even if it is a bit sickening. Sneaking in with a dagger and then skilfully slicing into a fellow's belly is just simple enough human behaviour. That's just man's way with his neighbour. (That was even man's way with His Saviour, when I remember Jesus and Calvary.) Very simple to understand Ehud and Eglon.

And Barak is much the same, when I remember that exploding star and that cosmic "dust" and the wonder of Your way with the machinery You have built into a thunderstorm. Yes, Barak makes sense, even if it has to be Heaven-sized sense. But, God—for I am still talking to God, I must talk to God—this is just suicide. Even if those three hundred water-pots were filled to the brim with gun-cotton or napalm or even atomic energy, it's still the same—curtains! Dear God, I know Gideon thinks You can do it. Do You think he's trusting You to flash some fire and burn the Arabs up like the fire that burned that kid and those unleavened cakes? Something like that, Gideon must be expecting. But I'm twentieth century. We know most of the basic mechanism of the whole universe, and where can You, even You, find one this size?

But God doesn't answer me. There is no answer. There is no sound at all. I am left there, sitting on a rock on the hillside where I last saw Gideon before the shadows swallowed him up. It is the silence of night. A cricket chirrupping, a few leaves rustling in the light breeze. Away across the Arab camp comes the faint stamp of a horse's hoof, the strange grunt of a camel as it is disturbed in its sleep. The sounds are those of night, of sleep, of an army at rest.

And then there is a slight stirring. A few half-whispered words, the tread of men moving quietly but not stealthily— I recognise it immediately—they are changing the guard. The short disturbances that will probably give that Arab another nightmare, I think to myself, the sort of disturbance the patients complain about, as the night supervisor makes her round with the floor duty nurse. In a minute it will be still again, silent, night, dawn still several hours away, time for long, easy sleep ...

Crash! Bellow! Pandemonium!

Who can ever describe it? Even Hollywood has never tried this one. It's the unbelievable end.

For as the first harsh blare of a ram's horn cut the night air, the whole hillside seemed to blow up. Three hundred earthenware jars were hurled crashing on to the rockface, three hundred torches waved in flashing arcs from inside the jars where they had been completely hidden until then, three hundred trumpets blared into a wild, raucous out-of-tune cacophany, and three hundred human throats fairly burst with the screaming, bellowing war-cry, "A sword for the Lord and for Gideon!"

And the waving torches, the blaring trumpets, the human shouting, were lost. They were as nothing!

For over the whole vastness of the Arab camp came something that was absolutely shattering. It was the screaming terror of panic. The panic of the camels. Those mighty "ships of the desert", those proud and vaunted transport mounts of the Arab army—the camels were stampeding!

Oh, God, I am half-shouting, half-crying, what incredible wonder is this? As the whole camp is now a sheer maelstrom of death and confusion, the simplicity of it is as great as the awe of it. Here was I, thinking of meteors and atomic power and even napalm and gun-cotton. And all the time. You knew something altogether else—You knew the psychology of the camel. You designed the camel.

And I am shouting now, in unashamed exultation and delight, as the thunderous turmoil in the encampment gains more and more momentum. For I am not exulting in order to egg on the ghastly death that is now carving its bloody way through the whole scene, any more than I am delighting in the destruction of a cruel, bitter invasion force. No. I am shouting in the wonder of the mind of God, exulting in the delight of knowing how utterly aware God is of all the precise details of His creation.

Was there ever a night like this? As Arab fell on Arab, as friend killed friend, as tent-mate mowed down tent-mate, as in it all and over it all and through it all thundered the flailing hooves of myriad bolting camels?

Yes, was there ever a victory like this one? As Gideon, fast-thinking, far-seeing Gideon rallied his men, as his messengers dashed across country· to call back the troops despatched home to take the Jordan crossing and cut off all hope of escape for the annihilated Arab war machine—who can ever even picture a story like this one?

Oh, God, I am saying—and surely this time I am really praying—I think I see it now as I have never seen it before. Barak was simple, and the lesson is simple. He heard Your voice say, "This is the day", and he went. No queries, no clues, no imaginative planning, just the simple, unquestioning obedience of servant to master, of disciple to Lord. Wonderful, thrilling. That's why I want so much to be like Barak, to have his simple directness of trust.

But Gideon—oh, God, Gideon is fantastic. In the awe of sheer reverence, I must say it: *You* are fantastic. That alert mind of Gideon's, that question-filled brain, that tremendous imagination—all of that You knew, You understood, You made. And this is in fact what You demanded. You asked for the whole of Gideon, mind, questions, imagination and all. Gideon, You were asking, come, follow me. I'll instruct your mind, I'll extend your imagination, I'll answer your questions—I want you altogether.

Dear Lord, I know I am right in this: I know Gideon had that whole campaign mapped out in his mind before he first started out. He knew it was right, because he knew he was at peace with You. And those 32,000 men were hopelessly too many. And so were the 10,000. He needed only a few hundred. Enough to set up three small companies, one on each of the three ridges coming down to the plains—all of this he knew. It was brilliant, it was genius. But, God, he didn't know the camels. Camels were new in his world. He didn't know, as we know so well today, how touchy a camel is, how gingerly it needs to be handled. He was trained in oxen, stolid, stubborn beasts that are hard enough to shift with a bulldozer—he knew nothing about camels. But he knew about *You*. And every part of him was utterly and altogether obedient to Your voice. That's why he is in Heaven's Roll, that's why he is one of the great men of faith.

I know now, if ever I knew, how much of a man You are concerned with. You are concerned with everything! The lot. His simple humanity, if he is a Barak; but his most complex capacities if he is a Gideon. All of it. No part of it may stay outside Your claim. That's what Gideon has shown me. And that is really what I want, too. That is what I am asking. In Your love and in Your divine generosity, will you please accept this, all of this, from John Hercus?

My publisher has kindly left a space between this paragraph and that last one—that paragraph that tried to express the simple, heart-deep prayer that just burst out of me as I saw the incredible miracle of the stampeding camels.

But the space as you see it in print gives no real indication of the space in the writing of the manuscript. For it is nearly a year since I wrote about Gideon and the Arabs and the camels. About Gideon and God, Gideon with God. And here I am, pen in hand again, going on with his story.

I didn't want to, I admit. A story like Gideon's, with its finished and rounded-off finality, has said all it can say. It's all done, the war's over, we can just demob and toss away our army kit and go back again to good old Civvy Street normal.

That's what I thought, that's certainly what I felt.

But that is not what God has recorded. For in the limitless patience of His teaching, God has taken up the story of Gideon again. And so, reluctantly, after nearly twelve months, hesitantly, I'm back in the picture ...

The last I saw of Gideon, as the thunder of camels' hooves drowned all other sensation from my mind, was as he rallied his tiny force, whipped off runners to the remainder of his previous army to call them to hold the Jordan passes—and he himself was dashing east to join in the final rout of the Arabs.

But as I read on, I see that there was in fact a lot more to it than that. For his rallying call did not just reach the remainder of his former troops—it carried right through the hills of Naphtali and Asher, as well as all his own tribe of Manasseh.

Even further still. For Gideon's was that alert, lightning-fast brain that could think the move beyond the move beyond the next. And up into all the hill country of Ephraim went the same message—"Quickly! I've got the whole Arab army on the run. Come and help finish them off. Can your men seize all the waters as far as Beth-barah, as well as the Jordan? Cut off all major water supplies and we've got the camel troops at our mercy. Quickly, please, now's our chance to do it together, and do it completely."

Out streamed the massed strength of Ephraim, the largest but least united of all the tribes, and they pounced down on the fleeing Arabs—and captured the two chief sheiks.

Oreb and Zeeb, these two Bedouin princes were, and they killed them both. And as at last Gideon and his weary men came jogging up, there were the two corpses of their previous oppressors.

But the Ephraimites were not a bit happy. In fact they were simply boiling. "You miserable little punk, just what do you think you've been doing? Going out and tackling the desert invaders without even consulting us first. What lousy sort of way is this to start a war? Somebody ought to whip some sense into that stupid skull of yours."

Shades of U.N.O. and the dear old defunct League of Nations. Not to mention the whole of the diplomatic corps.

Gideon was staggered, and well he might be. But not for a single fleeting moment did he show it. As fast as lightning, but as soft as thistledown, came his answer. "Oh, gentlemen, you are really over-rating me. I'm only a very small operator, and well do I know it. I've just been lucky with the breaks, but it's you fellows who have earned the lion-sized praise. Look at your bag compared with mine—I've knocked a bit of a hole in the Arab invasion force, I realise, but it's you and your men who have got the kings themselves. It's you who got Oreb and Zeeb."

And with a quick smile and a final word of thanks and congratulation he was on his way again.

What a man! Human genius doesn't come in much higher ratings than Gideon's. No wonder God checked out on Gideon so carefully and with such subtle attention to detail. A man with all that agility of mind and so much tenacity of purpose, as well as such charm of manner—that man needs the most careful watching, if he is to avoid mistaking his own will for God's will.

But I have no time to reflect, and Gideon and his men have no time even to stop for a snack—they're on their way again. Across the Jordan, now, hot on the heels of Zebah and Zalmunna, the two remaining Arab sheiks ...

In spite of the fatigue and hunger that now began to dog them, they raced down to Succoth. But too late. The Arabs had gone by.

The men of the town came out and stared at the clatter-
ing troops who staggered into Succoth, tired, dusty, dishevelled. Of course they had not had the advantage of a morning
news-flash on their transistors to tell them of Gideon's success, the morning newspapers had not broken with the story
—the stare was hard and long.

"Gentlemen, can you give me a bit of help, please? I and
my men have got the whole Arab invasion force on the run,
and we're now hot on the scent of Zebah and Zalmunna.
But we're famished. Could you give us a bit of food please?
We've been going all day yesterday and pretty well right
through the night, and if we're to catch those Arabs we'll
need a few more calories all round. Can you help us?"

The stare in the eyes and faces of the locals became
slightly more set. There was that barely perceptible narrowing of eyelids that warns the poker player to look out for
strength. And there was a silence, that awkward silence, that
summing-up silence, which in a modern business conference is provided by the pause to take a sip from a glass, the
time to light up a pipe or cigarette—that sort of silence.
Then the mayor spoke. Slowly, quietly. In a good film this
tiny "bit" part could perhaps go to a tall, drawling Texan—
"Sorry, mister, we're right glad to hear what you have to
say. Real glad. And we'll be mighty pleased to help you,
see, mighty pleased. So what say you keep right along on
the trail of these two sheiks, Zebah and Zalmunna, and
when you've caught up with them, and then when you've
roped them good and proper, bring them right back and
we'll do you real proud. We'll turn on a regular fine civic
Thanksgiving Dinner just for you. Hot roast turkey, cranberry sauce and all the trimmings. Yes, mister, you do just
that. Fetch those two Arab critters back and we'll be waiting
for you. Mister, you've got a good day's work ahead of you,
that's plain to see, so you'd better get those men of yourn
right back on the desert road, and we won't hold you up
even for a cup of coffee. Good day to you, mister."

Sure, I can imagine how Hollywood would play it. But I

can also imagine how Gideon felt when Succoth did in fact play it.

Gideon's face was a study in the conflict of elation and fatigue and humiliation. But his self-discipline and grim determination held back the explosion that looked so inevitable. His own words had a matched quiet, unhurried emphasis. "Well, gentlemen, that sounds very hospitable of you. I'm sure I and my men will be more than glad to take up that offer of yours, and join in your celebration party. And we'd like the privilege of contributing a little to the feast. What say we bring back something from the desert also? Something besides Zebah and Zalmunna? We'll bring back some lovely big spiky cactus plants, and a few sturdy briar vines with plenty of nice big sharp prickles on them. And then as we eat your hot roast turkey and cranberry sauce, you can have a good hearty taste of our thorns and prickles. You can count on it. Good day!"

And he wheeled his mount and raced on. And the half-hearted guffaws from the men of Succoth were lost in the clatter of hooves and the half-smirking faces were hidden in the cloud of dust.

On, still on. Still out towards the desert, across the Jabbok river, to Penuel. But Penuel was no more help than Succoth. "Food? Sure, we'll have plenty of food ready for you when you come back from capturing Zebah and Zalmunna. Plenty of food. What do you say to a big civic dinner on the top of our tower? It's a splendid tower, don't you think? We haven't got a revolving restaurant, we admit, and the elevators are not quite the most high-speed automatic models, but it's still a glorious cool spot for a real slap-up civic dinner. We're looking forward to it."

Gideon's temper and patience were straining thinner. This time there was no banter in his reply, there was no hint of answering in mock mirth. Just a sharp, terse, "I'll be back, and you can count on it. And when I do come back, and my mission is successfully accomplished, I'll break this tower down. Right down. Good day."

The Arabs were back in the desert, of course. Back on

the desert "shore". And Gideon's clear, far-seeing mind and
tactics pin-pointed them at Karkor. Hungry, exhausted,
humiliated by his own people, Gideon still never faltered.
Flanking and encircling the small Arab remnant, he followed
the caravan route to Jogbehah and swept in from the desert.
Again deploying the so-successful ruse of sheer surprise
attack, he and his men routed and decimated the Bedouins.
And Zebah and Zalmunna, the two remaining Arab chiefs,
were taken . . .

Smart fellow, this Gideon, and make no mistake about
that. Really smart. I said earlier how sure I was that he had
had the whole of that midnight surprise attack on the Midianite host clearly in his mind before the prophet even met
him. But Gideon is one of God's men, and he had checked
and rechecked with God before putting that original plan
into effect.

But this mopping-up campaign is very different. It doesn't
call for that far-sighted imagination that stampeded the
camels, it needs the quick-thinking alertness that will follow
up any sudden new lead, and it certainly needs the tenacious
doggedness that will stick to it in spite of the greed of
Ephraim and the churlish un-neighbourliness of Succoth
and Penuel. And Gideon had all of these. A tremendous
array of personal gifts.

And I am wondering even more, now. For I am wondering
about God. Gideon hasn't said a word to God since that
raucous, middle-of-the-night, three hundred voice shout, "A
sword for the Lord and for Gideon." Not a word. I ask
myself, is it really true that he's checking out with God
all the time, in fact, and the historian hasn't bothered to
tell us about it? Is the writer just taking it all for granted,
assuming that we will all realise that of course Gideon is
checking with God, checking on himself, with a wet and
dry fleece, etc. Or—and this "or" is what disturbs me—is
Gideon just playing it by ear, and is he assuming that
because God supported his one main scheme, that therefore
God will tag along with all his schemes?

I don't know. But I'm bothered. For I know how closely a man, any man, even Christ Himself, needs to keep tuned in to the Voice of God. God, who literally knows the end from the beginning, is the one who knows every turning in the right path in life. And when a disciple finds clear instruction to travel to the east, for example, he need not be at all surprised to discover that part of that road may in fact be heading due west. No, that should be no surprise. For that loop in the road was hidden from his sight, foot-slogging it down the dusty track, and the twists and turns are part of the straight course that is really taking him to his home—but how often must he need to enquire again and again, to make sure that he is in fact on the proper road. Yes, indeed, this is just part, a very real and important part, of being a disciple.

So I'm back following Gideon, following with a slight question mark, as he comes rolling back across the desert border, Zebah and Zalmunna now captives at his side.

I'm wondering whether Gideon has forgotten Succoth and Penuel.

I'm wondering what he will do with the two Arab princes.

I'm wondering a lot of things ...

He came back by a different road, I noticed—he climbed in by the Heres road—and he had me guessing. But not for long. For by the roadside he found a youth whom he dragged in for questioning. And sure enough, the lad was from Succoth. And he extracted from the poor kid the names of all the chief aldermen and big burgomasters and top merchants in the township. Seventy-seven names, in all, he got out of that kid. Some kid. I have no doubt that the average Aussie youngster would be able to reel off quite a list of names of cricketers and pop-singers and footballers and the like, but to name even our Governor-General or Prime Minister would very likely prove near to impossible—let alone the names of the mere local government gentry and business magnates. But the fellow from Succoth gave Gideon seventy-seven.

No, Gideon had not forgotten Succoth. He most certainly had not! And as his little army came bursting into the township, there was Gideon out in front, holding up his list of the seventy-seven-men-I-want-to-meet-but-who-do-not-want-to-meet-me. For as Gideon rounded them all up, his men came behind him, waving the big thorny cactus plants and the sinewy, prickly briar canes from the wilderness. A very unusual civic luncheon party indeed, I should say, with Zebah and Zalmunna right there in the middle, the main side-show of that ghastly occasion.

And then Penuel, too. Down crashed their tower, the skulls of the poor wretches inside cracked open in the collapse.

My, but there are some horrible ways to die, I'm thinking ...

So finally home to Ophrah, back to his own town and village. Zebah and Zalmunna are still with him, still carrying themselves with all the dignity and aloofness of men marked out for death, but men still able to laugh and quip in the very shadow of the grave.

I am wondering just what on earth Gideon is up to, bringing these two Arabs all the way back here. But I understand Gideon too well now to be imagining that he's just waiting for some bright idea to turn up, wondering what on earth he should do with them in the end. Not Gideon. He's got his scheme, you may be sure.

And surely enough, at last, at Ophrah, in the presence of his family, out came the whole thing. There they were, Zebah and Zalmunna standing tied together, as Gideon and his family faced them.

"Tabor? You remember Tabor?" Gideon's few words had a whiplash bite in them.

The Arab princes glanced at each other. "Yes, Gideon ..." one of them started to speak.

"Prince Gideon," corrected the other.

"Yes, Prince Gideon." The bow and the title hid none of the aloof contempt the Arabs felt for their unknown upstart conqueror. "Yes, we remember Tabor. Remember it well."

There was a curl of his lip and a sneer in his voice. But Gideon passed that by. His words were hot, passionate, tense —"Where are they? The men you took at Tabor, where are they now?"

Gideon wasn't taking this lightly, whatever it was. He was brittle, brittle to breaking-point. But the Arabs were still superbly indifferent and casual. "Oh, those men at Tabor? Well, now, what a pity about them. Sure, we remember now. They looked very like you, you know, now we stop and think about it. Very like you. In fact, now that you mention it, you and they would look like peas in a pod. Incredible likeness, now we really turn our minds to it. The same high, noble princely qualities." And this time they both bowed low in their mockery and scorn.

Gideon's face was white, his lips were trembling, his words came with difficulty. "Those men were my brothers. My own older brothers. If you had let them stay alive I would have spared you. Jether!" He turned to a leggy adolescent lad standing there, rather white of face, watching it all. Jether was Gideon's own eldest child. "Jether, you get a sword and come and kill these two devils!"

I saw the Arabs' faces blanch just for a second. This kid would hardly be big enough and strong enough to carve his way into their vitals, and I could see that the prospect of this horrible chop-and-hack death was as fearful as the sheer ignominious humiliation of death at the hand of a mere child.

But it was Jether who saved them. His face went ash-white, his lips began to tremble, I thought he would vomit in another moment. Gideon recognised the panic, and so did the Arabs.

"Looks as though it's up to you, after all, old man." Zebah said it as tantalisingly and yet as resignedly as if he were asking the wicket keeper to bowl from the Randwick end.

And Zalmunna chimed in with a superbly satirical sneer: "That's if you're strong enough, of course."

And so Gideon killed them, princes to the very end. And Gideon took as personal mementos the beautiful crescent-shaped ornaments that were hanging so richly from their camels' necks.

Hmmm. I'm saying to myself, Gideon may be a very smart man, but these Arabs were princes. Real princes. They showed Gideon something of the poise and self-disciplined courage that only great experience in rulership may bring to any man. I hope it doesn't give him ideas. I hope it doesn't make him think he should start a dynasty, set up as a ruler.

No, it didn't give Gideon any such idea. But it did give it to some of his followers. For the grunts and the whispers and the little groups in earnest conclave one day all came to a head. "Gideon," burst out their spokesman, "what say you become our ruler? How about being our king? Then your son could take over from you and his son from him. What do you say to that? You've earned it, beating the Bedouin like that, and it would suit us all fine."

I chuckled as I heard it—I wondered to myself just what the Ephraimites would think of the scheme. I wondered how many votes came from Succoth and Penuel. I smiled wryly as I saw Gideon's alert mind catch the full implications of the request.

But I need not have feared. "Gentlemen, I appreciate your offer, but I couldn't think of it. I just won't even consider being your ruler, and neither will my son after me. *God* will be our ruler."

It was said simply, yet firmly, clearly. But not in any sense reluctantly or bitterly. I almost felt like calling for three cheers, not cheers for Gideon, but cheers for God. For God and Gideon. What a trap, I was thinking, what a simple trap and yet what a deadly trap. How fortunately Gideon escaped it. He can thank them if he likes—he seems to be getting ready to say something—and then they can all go home and he can go back to Joash and talk about the replacement plans for the number two bull, and all the other things that make up a humble farmer's life.

Yes—Gideon is speaking—he has in his hands the two beautiful ornaments from Zebah and Zalmunna's camels. He's fingering them nervously, he's obviously slightly embarrassed. What can be in his mind?

Listen: "Yes, thank you, men. I do appreciate all you have already done, and most of all the kind and generous offer you have just made. I know how sincerely you intend it"—Gideon stopped and glanced around. His words had been very simple, almost trite, much like the standard speech-in-reply of any such official or political meeting. But the earnestness, the slight hesitancy of actual words, showed how far from commonplace it all really was. And now his words were absolutely super-charged with intense emotion as he went on. "I should like to make a suggestion of my own. Would you be willing to make a gift of the earrings of your captives? Just a personal gift, and I'll do something worthwhile with them. Any of you interested? Do I have any takers? Would you be willing to do that?"

It was a bombshell. It almost lifted them off their feet. Those earrings were the most fabulous, unbelievable, out-of-this-world treasures these poor hilltop people would ever set eyes on and here he was asking them to unclasp their hands and deliberately allow such wealth to slip from their grasp. There was a pause, a silence, that was more dramatic than any roaring and shouting and yelling could ever produce. Only a few seconds of time, but the sort of few seconds that can contain an absolute age of feelings and concern.

My own mind was racing. A whole world of doubts and questions chased each other through my mind. He's not going to splurge it all in a great big beano, Gideon's not the high-living, wild-party type. And he's not the hoarder who will just salt it all away for his own good to be available in some later rainy day experience. Just what is it he has in mind? Surely he's not—oh, no, not Gideon. Gideon won't be so silly as to go and use it all on some great big public display programme, with his name plastered all over it for admirers to stare at—"Gideon unveiled this monument in commemoration of his victory over the Arabs"; "The Gideon War Memorial"; "Deo et Gideoni" and all that human nonsense. No, Gideon won't do anything like that. I wonder. And I wonder ...

Something in me wants to call out and warn Gideon. I know he hasn't stopped to speak a single word to God, he hasn't made one tiny move to check it all out with God— I just know he has some scheme buzzing away inside that brilliant mind of his. Some scheme that is entirely his own. No message from God about it in the slightest degree. Oh, Gideon, I begin to mutter, be very careful, I live in an age when man-made ideas weigh us down to the very depths of ignorance. Gideon, don't be so crazy as to start something you can't stop. Be more than careful ...

But I can't make myself heard, for now his men are coming up to him. There are tears in their eyes—but there are earrings in their hands. Yes, they are giving them over to Gideon. "Here you are, Gideon," they are saying, "you can have them. We will willingly give them."

"So a cloak was spread out and every man threw on to it the golden earrings from his booty. The earrings for which he asked weighed seventeen hundred shekels of gold; this was in addition to the crescents and pendants and the purple cloaks worn by the Midianite kings, not counting the chains on the necks of their camels. Gideon made it into an ephod and he set it up in his own city of Ophrah. All the Israelites turned wantonly to its worship, and it became a trap to catch Gideon and his household."

God is fair, more than fair, in His dealings with men. And nowhere more fair that in His account of the story of Gideon. Gideon is himself in the eleventh chapter of the Epistle to the Hebrews, his name is on that greatest Honours Roll ever compiled. But God is still fair enough to tell us the whole story. Not just the account of what God can do with the brilliant, gifted, superb accomplishments of a man when all those qualities are in His will, but also the sad, nation-destroying problems that arise when the man, even

the same man, sets out to go it alone. For the obedience
that is faith, real faith, is never coerced, it is never compulsion. Faith is that utterly unique relationship of a man to his
God in which the man deliberately wills the will of God.
And how easy, how terribly easy it is for a man like Gideon,
with ideas just buzzing in his head all the time, to forget,
clean forget, how essential it is for him to put all those ideas
under the scrutinising lens of the declared will of God.

Yes, God is everything that is fair, as He goes on to tell
us what happens when Gideon fails to check it all out with
God. You can read, if you have such a mind to read, the
whole blood-drenched story of the human hatefulness that
follows so dramatically when men lose their clear, meaningful contact with the will of God. When men get their contact with God through the man-made medium of a mere
ephod. Read of Abimelech. Abimelech, son of a slave-wife.
Abimelech, who inherited so much of his father's genius,
but who inherited none—for it is never inherited—of his
father's faith. Abimelech, who murdered sixty-nine of his
seventy brothers. Abimelech, who was himself struck down
by a millstone dropped on his skull by a woman.

Yes, you can read it if you like, there in the ninth and
tenth chapters of the Book of Judges. There it stands for all
time, one of the most solemn warnings ever recorded, to
teach men to avoid this tragic mistake: the mistake of
Gideon when he did *not* check it all out with God.

Yes, indeed, read if you have such a desire, in the Book
of Judges. But I will be reading it on the front of any newspaper I care to open. That front page news which splashes
across the top of page one. The headline news of riot and
arson and rape and murder, at home; and of war and more
war and more war still, abroad. The assassination of a
Kennedy and of a Martin Luther King—and of another
Kennedy. The firing of huge cities and the students in
revolt. The clash of arms and the spurting of blood—blood
of fellow-countryman and of man-across-the-street. That's
what I read, any day now, every day now. Not reading it in
the Book of Judges, but reading it in the daily paper. For the

laws of social man are as inflexible and as inexorable as the laws of gravity or any other of the laws of God. And if perhaps it took a Freud or a Bowlby to begin to realise that such laws do exist, today the whole ghastly pattern of breakdown is open for any to learn.

So that if you read the story in the Book of Judges you will find that for Gideon it meant fame and honour and wealth; while for his home and family and nation it meant almost unparalleled horror.

And if I read the story in the daily newspaper I will find the same; the very same thing. It's a story of achievement and wealth and prosperity; but a story of disaster and collapse and disillusionment.

For in spite of his faith, Gideon built an ephod. Just an ephod. And in spite of the very presence of God in the life of Man, we have built a religion. Just a religion ...

And that is the story of Gideon. That is what God is really telling us in such starkly contrasting examples. It is the story of the greatest marvel in the experience of man: the marvel of a relationship with God in which a man may expect to know the will of God for any single event or decision in life. But it is also the story of the greatest disaster in human affairs: the disaster of human behaviour when it is isolated from the will of God.

So that I am at last speaking to myself. It is John Hercus, that ordinarily successful medical practitioner in this late twentieth century: John Hercus, God wants you altogether. Every single bit of you. Not just your religion and your time of worship and church attendance, but all the routine run-of-the-mill commonplace matters that make up so much of life. And even those newest operating techniques and the vague research ideas—yes, and also the most personal and intimate secrets of home and family and your inmost self—God demands the lot. John Hercus, there cannot be a single tiny area of life in which you are not to check it out with God.

How much of his being does God want in a man? Gideon

tells us the exciting answer: all of him. Gifts, imagination, mind, personality—the lot. And for how long does God ask these of a man, for what length of time? Gideon tells us the warning answer: all the time, all of time.

JEPHTHAH

"Jephthah the Gileadite was a great warrior."

That is the heading to the story of the next man we will be looking at. And I take a deep breath and lick my lips and wonder just what this will produce. My ears are still tingling and my head still spinning from the thunderous roar and the death-beat of the hooves of the stampeding camels thrown into panic by Gideon—and we first saw him as a hide-away grain grinder in a wine-press in Manasseh. That's all Gideon was to start with. But Jephthah is "a great warrior".

And I remember Barak—can I ever possibly forget Barak? —and the stupendous victory God gave to this simple yokel. My goodness, if this can happen to Barak, just think what may turn up when we start with a great warrior in the starring role. This should be quite a story.

Then there was Ehud and his dagger. Sure, Ehud was a solo worker, he didn't trust anybody—but he was an assassin right from the start of the story. He didn't whisper a single hint of the murderous secret strapped to his right thigh. Ugh! That was surely one tough little *hombre*, and no mistake about that! Then if Ehud is a lone-wolf sample of the species, think what the story of a great warrior may tell us. This is likely to be the story of all stories about blood and thunder and all such military mayhem.

My, but I'm interested. Let me read on quickly.

And I read. And I read. And I read ...

I wonder what it is? I don't seem to be able to concentrate or something. I'm missing the point of the story, it seems. Perhaps it's these bifocals, perhaps they need changing—must see about getting a new pair, I've had them about five years, perhaps that's the trouble. I'll come back later. I think I'll stop for a game of tennis and help blow the cobwebs away or something like that. I'll come back later and read it again.

And I re-read. And I re-read ... And I re-read ...

And I'm bewildered. Lost ... Something is still missing. It's not my bifocals—they're good for another three or four years. I'm not tired or upset or preoccupied or distracted or worried. No nothing like that.

It's the story that is the trouble. The story of Jephthah the Gileadite who was the great warrior—that's what is wrong.

Oh, sure, there is a bit of scrapping in it, a little border clash between the tribespeople of Gilead and the indigenous Ammonites who co-existed so uncomfortably right alongside them. And the Ephraimites get pretty severely trounced in the process, and we do see something of the stern strength and relentless toughness of Jephthah as he thrashed them. Yes, I see all that. But nothing of the Gideon–Arab drama, no tiny hint of the Barak–Sisera saga. Small, scrappy, two-bit parochial stuff. Nothing Big Name; local history, not world history.

And yet there it is: "Jephthah the Gileadite was a great warrior." Splashed clean across the top of the two chapters that tell us all we know about him, there stands the headline announcement. I can't miss it and I don't miss it. I'm not misreading it, either. Certainly I'm not imagining it: "Jephthah the Gileadite was a great warrior."

I think how we would write this today. How we did write it not many years ago: "Churchill on Job"; "Churchill takes over"; "D-Day in Normandy"; "Ike in Charge". I remember my dad saying the same thing of an earlier day: "Lloyd George Visits Trenches"; "Foch in Supreme Command".

And there it is, just the very same thing: "Jephthah now C-in-C", "Gileadite warrior in Command".

Yes, the headlines are there, unmistakably there, I haven't mistaken the headlines. But the story is not there. It's not that sort of story at all. What on earth shall I do?

And even as I ask myself the question, even as I say the words, I know the answer. There is nothing on earth to be done, for the answer is not on earth at all, it is in Heaven. God alone can explain this story. This is not the daily newspaper, this is not a bit of tawdry human journalism, this is not eye-catching poster material—no, this is the writing of God, this is the voice of Heaven. God doesn't work in 72-point headlines. He isn't writing to attract the buying-interest of the casual passer-by. God is not standing by the sidewalk of life calling a raucous "Paper, sir?", "Buy a paper, sir?", "Read all about it! Special late war news. Buy a paper, sir?"

And I bow my head and humble my heart as I start to read again. This great Gileadite warrior—what is God telling us in his life that will teach us about Himself and His will? That is the real question—nothing at all to do with drama and excitement and entertainment and mere passing news. Instruction, God is writing, not information.

For God is going to start the story by taking us to the life of a man who is just a great warrior. But, be assured, God is going to finish the story by showing us something of what it means to be a man of faith.

And Jephthah was this great warrior.

Now there is no particular secret today in understanding how a man becomes a great warrior. Three ingredients are needed, and three only. If you have them, then you are likely to become a great warrior.

Firstly, you will need some good human equipment in terms of brain or male aggressiveness ("drive", if you prefer the euphemism) or sheer physical toughness; secondly, sufficient emotional conflict to keep pounding away inside you so relentlessly that it will forever prevent you from feeling satisfied, fulfilled, at peace; and thirdly, a job or vocation or racket which will give you the scope to express your churned-up feelings to their full, well-equipped limits.

And Jephthah had all three.

He got the first from his father. Dad was the tribal leader or chieftain. You couldn't be tribal boss in those days unless you had the ginger to back it up. Dad was the leader.

And he got the second from his mother. Mother was a prostitute, Jephthah was a bastard. Surely there's enough conflict in a wretched start in life like that. Surely!

And for the third ingredient Jephthah had all the scope in the world, for he was a bandit. Yes, that's what I said—a bandit. The genuine, flint-hard, throat-slitting, raiding bandit. Grade A, too. A successful bandit.

There he is: son of the tribal chief; illegitimate bastard; bandit. And God chose him, God picked this fellow. Jephthah is one of those altogether illustrious men of faith God has named in His roll of honour. Just how on earth will Heaven perform a wonder like this? What can God be seeing in this sort of man to accept him as His own?

Now please don't get the idea that I'm suggesting that this role of great warrior comes to a man just as easily as kiss-your-hand. Don't imagine that it's just a knack that Jephthah was lucky enough to have been born with. Not one tiny bit of it.

This prowess of Jephthah's was the result of bitter, tragic, heart-tearing conflict and hatred that dated from his infancy. He was learning to fight, and fight to win, almost before he could run. For strangely enough, his father kept him, illegitimate and bastard and all that he was, while the poor prostitute who actually bore him was sent packing. And as his father's wife bore sons, "proper", "legitimate" sons, Jephthah became their bait, their hated rival, the object of their collective scorn.

"Ha! Ha! Ha! Look at silly Jephthah." "His mother doesn't live here! She isn't our mother." "Jephthah, Jephthah, look at silly Jephthah!" Nice little half-brothers, normal little half-brothers, chanting their childhood cruelty and their boyhood brutality as they romped and played and kicked the hopscotch in the hot Gileadite sun. Nice little half-brothers. Yes, normal little half-brothers.

"Hey! Jephthah, you! Buzz off! You don't belong here, bastard! There's nothing for you here, see? This is our place. You keep your distance. Only us proper sons own this place. Not you. Scram!"

Yes, that's how it went. That's how it must go, sons and
bastards alike, in the home where lust had displaced love.

And as the unsought baby grew into the unwanted boy
growing into the unacceptable youth, Jephthah knew what
it meant. It meant out. It meant run. It meant an end, a
bitter, cruel, sad, merciless end to any wistful, tear-filled
dreams of home and warmth and affection. It meant the time
had come to go.

The fact that his father was the chieftain meant nothing.
Nothing at all. Nothing good at all. It just meant that the
taunts and the rivalry and the hatred had more meaning.
There was more to lose.

But there was no other answer. If he didn't stand up to
them and just beat them into submission, the only thing
to do was to escape. And the kid who just keeps running
his face up against the hate-driven fists of all the others in
the place isn't going to make a great warrior. That stupid
kid just makes the pain more painful; he's just heading for
the casualty ward. No, Jephthah knew what to do.

"So Jephthah, to escape his brothers, went away and
settled in the land of Tob."

That is all the old Hebrew historian says. Into those fifteen
words he compresses all the wretchedness and the conflict
and the hell-on-earth misery that was the life of the baby,
the boy, the youth. "So Jephthah, to escape his brothers,
went away ..."

Now don't make any silly *Westward Ho!* or *Treasure Island*
sort of mistake about Tob. "I'm sorry, son, you'll have to go.
I can see that. But here's fifty thousand dollars. How about
buying a nice little sheep farm in the Canterbury Plains in
New Zealand? Get yourself set up decently, something like
that. Good luck." Oh, no! Not in Tob.

"There's a wool clipper down at the docks now, son.
She's sailing for Australia at the turn of the tide. I'm sorry
I can't do anything to help, but get yourself on board as a
forward hand and I'm sure you'll make your fortune in the
new colonies." No, oh, no! That was what made so much of
Australia's greatness, sure it was. But that's not Tob.

Tob country is hill country. It is the wild never-never of no-man's-land. It is bandit country.

And Jephthah became a bandit. Jephthah "swept up a number of idle men who followed him". That's all we are told. That's what God tells us about this man He has picked. The bastard has now become a bandit—God's man!

Don't you sometimes find God embarrassing? Embarrassingly direct, embarrassingly honest? I certainly do. Just think of this story if it were to be told today. Think how it would be served up in the history books. Think, if you like, how it is served up in the history books. Think of the buccaneering escapades on the high seas of some of the great sea-dogs of our British history. Pirates, that's what they really were, if our history books and boy's adventure stories were to tell us the simple truth. Greedy, ruthless, rogues. Yes: brave, and daring, and reckless of their own lives as of others; but still greedy, ruthless, rogues. And how many "great" men in history were really like this at heart? Is not much "greatness" in human experience in fact a summation of aggression, pride and greed?

But not Jephthah. Not when God tells the story. God just says: "So Jephthah, to escape his brothers, went away and settled in the land of Tob, and swept up a number of idle men who followed him."

Yes, that's how it reads: Jephthah "swept up a number of idle men who followed him". It wasn't a tale of a poor kid, there he was, hungry and destitute and friendless, just stumbled into a bandit lair one day, and the bandits took pity on him, gave him a bite to eat and some warm clothes and all against his fine noble instincts he got drawn inexorably into the evil ways of his wicked companions and so remember *Eric, or Little by Little*, and we will now conclude the meeting by singing hymn number 478, "Yield not to temptation".

What nonsense! What blasphemous nonsense! God is not writing a textbook of humanism or any other absurdity. He is telling us of His power to save.

Don't be surprised, then, don't be embarrassed, when you

read that Jephthah became the central figure. He was the leader who swept the idle men into his team. He was the Big Boss. Bandit. Bandit leader. Successful bandit leader.

Highly successful. Famous. People began to know of Jephthah and his cut-throats. That raiding party became a by-word for miles and miles around. Jephthah and his raiders. Bandits, successful bandits.

So successful that they heard of him back in Gilead. In his own tribe, in the very place where he had been so hated and despised, and where for at least a quarter of a century his name had just been forgotten, they were now speaking of him again. But now you didn't hear of Jephthah in words that were filled with taunting abuse and sneer-filled hatred: now it was in the bated breath and fear-filled whispers of respect. Until the very tribal leaders, his father's successor and the men who shared tribal leadership with him, heard of Jephthah, too. And what they heard stirred even deeper feeling still.

For the Gileadites were in strife. The Ammonites, this time. A little local across-the-border dust-up, that's all this was. Somewhere away out across the desert, up in the northeast, the gathering might of Assyria was just beginning to rock the whole of their world; but in this tiny Gileadite pocket that was still not the thing that troubled them. Their problem was the Ammonites.

Like the Moabites (and their fat king Eglon) the Ammonites were also descendants of Lot, and were really first cousins of the Israelites. But now there was a border-stealing tug-o-war going on, and the Gileadites were losing. Losing pretty badly, what's more. The Ammonites were putting it right over the Gileadites, who found that they were without a real leader. What they wanted was a good, tough, strong, experienced fighter who could argue and/or beat the Ammonites back across the Arnon and into their own national backyard.

And—yes, you've guessed it—they thought of Jephthah. Jephthah, the bandit. Jephthah, the successful bandit.

*   *   *

It's the road to Tob again. Up the winding, climbing, treacherous, precipitous, dangerous road to Tob. But not for Jephthah, not for the hated, lowly, outcast youth. No, it's the tribal leaders' turn now. Inching their way round the countless blind corners where death could lurk so easily, racing along the exposed tracks where sling-shot and arrow could flank so mercilessly, up the road to Tob. To Jephthah.

What a meeting! Years, now, many, many years, this has taken; but at last it has come to pass. Some faces white with fear, some faces red with confusion, but all faces bowed respectfully to the ground as they confronted Jephthah again.

Jephthah heard them out. Heard their tale of defeat by the Ammonites and their admission of weakness, their need for leadership. "That's our problem, sir, and now you have it. We're licked, and we need your help. Could you come and lead us against the Ammonites. Would you, sir? Please?"

Jephthah felt the pulse of anger rise in his temples, but he fought it back. His voice was quiet, too quiet, as he replied. "Yes, I see your problem. But I'm not sure that I see how it concerns me. You hated me, don't you remember? Really hated me. You turned me out of my father's house. I certainly remember that. Just kicked me out. And now you come to me when you are in trouble. I don't follow the logic of all this. Or is there no logic in it? What is there in it for me? Why should I be interested at all?"

The spokesman's voice was very subdued as he answered slowly. "Yes, sir. We realise that. But it's because we are in real trouble that we have come to you for help. We want you to come back and be our leader this time."

There was a long pause. That pause in which the alchemy of memory and the witchery of forgotten bonds may turn the bitter iron of hatred into the first glint of the pure gold of love. Jephthah's voice was very close to breaking as he answered simply. "If you take me back, back to my father's house, to join in your battle with the Ammonites, and if God gives me victory over them, then I will be your head."

I think it was the magic in the words "my father's house"

that did it. That was home, the home he had never had, had never known. The outcast mother could give him no home, for she had none herself; and his half-brothers had seen to it that he had no lot or part with them. But now it was to be home at last.

For Jephthah was married, and was a father. He had only one child, a lovely daughter, but she was now nearly woman, and here was the one and only chance of his life-time (and her lifetime, too) to get her a proper home.

Oh, sure, he was well enough dug in, up there in Tob. He was the bandit leader, his bandit lair was richly bedecked with the valuables and loot from his many successful raids. But not a home. Not a place in the close circle of kith and kin, not a place his lovely daughter should be growing up in. Where were her companions to come from, where was her future husband to come from, up in the fastness of Tob? From the children of the bandits, from the families of the worthless fellows who had collected round him in his raiding sorties? Could Tob ever be the "home" an only daughter should be allowed to grow up in?

I think I am right. I am sure I am right. "If you ask me back"—back to his father's house—that was what he had asked. It was they who spoke about going back; but it was he who spoke about "my father's house". That was Jephthah.

Yes, the illegitimate, outcast, hated bandit was at last to come home, to come home for the very first time in his life.

Yes, there were faces white with fear, there were faces red with embarrassment; but Jephthah's face was not white, not red—Jephthah's face was wet, as with quick blinking eyelids and furtive wiping by sleeve and hand the hot, well-ing tears were brushed away. Jephthah was on his way home.

And so it is the long Tob road once more, and Jephthah is again taking it. But this time it is for the last time, for it is the road back home. Jephthah is walking along beside his donkey-train. His wife is there, his only daughter is there. The journey takes days, crawling carefully and laboriously over the tricky passes, winding slowly round the blind corners where death may lurk in every shadow. I am thinking, pondering, wondering. This whole story seems so unreal, so close to fairyland fiction—I wonder if I can find any simple direct answers to my problem.

Jephthah has become separated a few yards from his family, and they are themselves separated a little from his tribesmen. Jephthah—I come up to him unhurriedly, unstealthily—I don't want his years of hair-trigger alertness to make him think I'm stalking him. Jephthah, I say again, falling into step beside him, this is a wonderful break, really. Sure, Jephthah, I know you have been treated terribly badly, getting kicked out as a lad when your father was the chief. That was a lousy deal if ever there was, and I know every fair-thinking person in the world feels genuinely sorry for you. We are all just thrilled to see how it has at last turned out. My own country of Australia has a lot of this sort of problem in its background, and there is no question that the intense reaction evoked by this sort of start in life is the explanation for some of the greatness we are now achieving.

Jephthah doesn't answer. I stop long enough for him to speak if he feels like replying, but his gaze is straight ahead, his lips do not even part for a second. He's not upset, he's thinking, too, I realise.

Slowly, quietly, I begin to speak again. I think I know how you feel; a bit, at any rate. I spend my whole life with people, Jephthah, and their feelings and their conflicts are really very much part of my workaday world. Do you have any plans already? What do you think your programme should be?

Jephthah spoke without turning to look at me at all. He was not a talkative, chatty sort of man—I thought quickly how he would irritate the modern press/T.V. interviewer who loves so dearly to get nice, pithy, "potted" answers— and his were short and reluctant. "I want to get home. Then I want to go to the watchtower, to Mizpah."

I didn't answer. I felt that Jephthah had something else to add. He stopped speaking, but these few enigmatic words had told me nothing. I waited for him to go on, to explain it. There are often times like this when I am speaking with my patients, times when they say something that opens a sudden glimpse into deep, poignant recesses of memory. I sensed that this was true of Jephthah now.

So that we were perhaps another two hundred yards on our way before he spoke again. "The watchtower in Gilead. I must go there."

Again that silence. But this time not so long. Jephthah turned at last and looked directly at me, speaking slowly, deliberately, every sign of intense, rigidly controlled emotion. "The watchtower is our special place of worship. I went there once. That was when I left home as a youth. I spoke to God then, and that was when I ran away. Now I want to go there again and speak to God again. Then I'll plan what comes next."

And his head snapped back from looking at me, he quickened his pace and lengthened his stride until in a very few moments we had closed the gap separating us from the rest of the party and the conversation was at an end.

I was satisfied. A few words, spoken with that simple direct honesty may often tell a doctor more than a full hour of reluctant equivocal answers. Jephthah was going home, but going home to God. At Mizpah, in the presence of the Lord, to repeat all that he had said.

I can sense the slight impatience in your mind as you read all this. "Jephthah the Gileadite was a great warrior" sounds like the heading for a really exciting story, you are thinking, and so far there isn't a single bit of hair-raising or blood-curdling in the whole thing. In fact it's all rather pathetic, banal, tear-jerking. Come on, let's assume he's got all this religious stuff straightened out, had his séance or whatever it is in Mizpah, the watchtower, and here he is, back as C-in-C of the Gileadite army. Now we'll see the great warrior in action. Come on, then, left, right, left, right, left, right, pick 'em up, march!

But not so fast. Remember, please, just who Jephthah was. Those thirty or forty years of banditry had taught Jephthah some quite unusual tactics. For every bandit knows that the very best profits in their trade come from negotiation. A lightning-strike coup which can pick up a single valuable hostage may show a greater net profit, may mean a ransom worth more trinkets and spending money, than a big pitched battle in which a whole convoy train is looted. Do a deal, try a bit of negotiation—that is the first rule in the book of words for banditry. You know the sort of thing: "I have got your son in custody as a hostage. I will release him immediately I receive $250,000 in small unmarked currency."

Jephthah tried it. "Some of your people have trespassed into our lands, seriously threatening peaceful co-existence. Why?" It was a typical bandit note, sharp, terse, to the point.

And I think how interesting it is to see how long this sort of thing has been going on. (Also interesting to see how remarkably accurate the old Bible stories remain, even after all these centuries of man-handling. Fancy the crazy judgment of people who say that they are all only "myth" and not really "happenings" at all. Fancy!)

So very much the same as today. These border demarcation disputes are always the same, then as now. "One of your planes was fifteen miles off course today and flew three miles into our country." "Shells from your artillery practice have been found on our side of the border." "Your fleets are fishing within our prescribed twelve mile limit."

Yes, you know the game, and you know the standard rules. A few heated words, some mild abuse, and the planes fly on course and the guns don't overshoot and the fishing fleets sail away. Back to *status quo*.

But not with the Ammonites. They were over the border because they intended to stay over that border, and that was just that. But their reply was still careful. They, too, preferred to negotiate. Their chief had a good answer ready. "I remind you that when your people of Israel came out of Egypt, you occupied all that part of our country in the Jordan Valley between the Arnon to the south and the Jabbok to the north. We are simply repossessing what is properly our own country, and we hope to do this peacefully."

A flat refusal.

Now however quick on the trigger a really good bandit may well be, he is never trigger-happy. So Jephthah took the time to do some careful research, backed by some quiet solid thinking, and forwarded another message. It is a masterpiece in diplomatic argument for anybody in that line of business. This is the gist of it:

"In reply to your last note, I must tell you that your facts are wrong, and thus you draw false conclusions. What really happened was this: When Israel came up out of Egypt, she travelled to the east of Palestine, which she planned to enter from the desert, not from the Mediterranean boundary. At Kadesh she stopped and asked permission from both the Edomites and the Moabites to travel through their lands. Israel did not move from Kadesh while awaiting their replies. In due time the answers came, and both Edom and Moab refused to allow her free passage. Israel respected and accepted these two refusals, and consequently detoured right out into the desert until she finally camped on the opposite banks of the Arnon; which, you note, is the boundary of Moab. At no time did Israel ever enter Moabite country.

"Israel then sent a message to Sihon, of Heshbon, asking yet again for free passage, this time through Amorite country. But the Amorite king did not even answer. He utterly rejected this peaceful and reasonable request and instead massed his troops and marched to the attack.

"Now you are fully aware of the outcome of that battle. For it was Yahweh, the God of Israel, who won that battle. He gave victory to His people, resounding victory, and all the Amorite land from the Arnon River to the Jabbok River fell into the possession of the victorious Israelite Army.

"The implication and the lesson is quite clear. Yahweh, the God of Israel, conquered that land. It is His, and He gave it to His people Israel.

"Then you do the same. Any land that Chemosh, your god, can conquer, is yours to take. But only that. Only the land he gives you. But certainly not the land Yahweh has given us. That is ours, and we are keeping it.

"Finally, may I remind you of Barak, king of Moab. He did not lift a finger in war against Israel. He was prudent. And remember further that all this happened ages and ages ago, and if you are naïve enough to think the Arnon–Jabbok territory is really still your own, then why have you waited all this ridiculously long time to repossess what you claim to be your own country?

"If there is war between you and me, it is war of your making, not mine. But it will be Yahweh, the Great Judge, who will decide this issue."

And so the gauntlet is down. But not the gauntlet of Gilead and Jephthah, the gauntlet of Gilead and God.

It is war. The negotiations have achieved nothing, the only answer left is battle. And Jephthah moves through all the tribe of Manasseh (of which Gilead is a large part) and draws his men together. I'm staying with him, you may be sure, now that this great warrior is in action. Right through his whole tribal area he is going, recruiting men for the campaign. Then moving out into the very limits of Manasseh, until he has his band complete. I'm wondering what tactical lines he will follow, which point he will attack first, whether he might throw a pincer grip around the Ammonites, or perhaps drive a sharp wedge into their main body and split their communication and fragment their forces. Jephthah got his training as a bandit, I remember, not in a Regular Army O.T.C.

And he's moving. Moving back into his own country, back—can this be true?—back to his home? Yes, he's coming back to Mizpah, where he has in fact settled down in his own home, just across a slight fall in the hillside from the watchtower itself.

This is superb, I'm saying to myself. It means a few more miles of foot slogging, but it's worth it just to see Jephthah visit his home again. He's been so long, so terribly long, finding a real home, that surely he's entitled to the chance of paying them a last short visit. A final kiss and word of farewell for his wife who has helped him so much in all those years in Tob. And a special hug for his daughter, his one and only child. I'll take the chance to get cooled off and have a last bit of a breather myself.

Yes, I'm right, he's halted his troops, they are resting for a short smoko, while Jephthah goes off by himself.

But it's not home he's heading for. It's that watchtower. He's not going to meet his family at all, he's going to meet his God.

And now I'm on my feet and dodging through the men sitting and lolling in the shade of the trees, I'm going to be there with Jephthah when he talks to God. Yes, I feel I must be there. For there is something that is worrying me, and now at last I can perhaps find my answer.

For I am worried by the thought of what Jephthah has been learning about God, all those long and wretched years in Tob. It is hard enough for an Australian today to learn anything very meaningful about God, and we have the whole of God's word available in every single city and suburban bookshop, in modern English for only a few dollars—and still nobody much seems to know. Even the religious leaders seem to have forgotten that there even is a textbook, much of the time, judging by the amazing statements they make and the even more amazing activities they get going. Gideon and his ephod is just the miniature scale-model by comparison.

But Jephthah has been in Tob. He has been in bandit country, just what will he have learned about God?

Jephthah is praying. He is standing, face upturned to the heavens, in the way so many people have prayed in many times; but there is a harshness, a stridor in his voice and speech that tells me just how tense is the emotion he is fighting back.

I'm standing just inside the narrow doorway to the watchtower, trying to quieten my heavy breathing after dashing up the little knoll. Listen! Listen to Jephthah.

"Yes, I promise You. I am trusting You to give me victory over the Ammonites. And if You do, I'll keep my bargain with You. I'll offer as a sacrifice the first person who comes out of the door of my house when I come back victorious. God, I promise You."

Oh, God! I can't believe it. God, did You hear that? Were You listening when he said that dreadful thing? Just what sort of a hell-on-earth must this Tob be, to give a man such a ghastly idea of what You are like, of what You do like? Fancy even thinking for a single moment that You might approve of human sacrifice. Oh, God, what utter wretchedness must exist in Tob. What a shocking distortion of truth.

But God—and I hardly dare even to whisper it to myself, let alone to God—God, suppose ... just suppose ... Oh, God ... and now I blurt it out—what say it should be a member of his actual family? What if it should be his daughter? God, please don't let him even risk it, don't even let him remember it again.

I feel sick with fear, simply racked by a horrible ghastly dread. But I haven't time to worry any longer, for Jephthah has brushed past me, striding down the slope to rejoin his army, a stern glint in his eye and a setting to his jaw that makes me tremble for the Ammonites when he catches up with them. Yes, I'm thinking, the Ammonites had better look out, with Jephthah with that look on his face.

It is hard to be sure just what happened in the campaign. I'm not too clear, the historian himself doesn't make it very clear. I don't think God wants it to be too clear, to tell you my real feelings. Oh, the battle was important, all battles are very important to the people fighting. And God knows that. But God is primarily concerned with man's relationship to Him; and tactics, deployment, manoeuvres and the like are to be judged in the light of that relationship.

I think Jephthah went in from the south. In a dramatic flanking forced march that completely skirted the whole of the Ammonite border, probably by the aid of some diversionary action up towards the north, it seems that Jephthah himself and his main army flooded in from the Arnon valley in the extreme south. He struck first at Aroer, and then advanced north in a three-thousand-year-old pattern of blitz-krieg until finally he sacked Minnith. Twenty little fortified towns fell in that advance, and Ammon was licked. It is also probable that most of the fighting men from all those tiny cities were away up in the north all the time, called up in the main Ammonite army. That is what I think happened.

Yes, I just think that is right, and I think it has the right sounding ring of bandit tactics that Jephthah would deploy so skilfully. I also think that he was still on his way home, mopping up the last pockets of Ammonite resistance, when the Ephraimites struck. Spurred on by greed and jealousy, his brother tribe of Ephraim had come over in hostile array, with the complaint that he should have been invited to the party, and with the open demand for a share in the booty. Yes, I think I am right in that.

But I am sure I am right in saying what happened to Ephraim. That stern glint in Jephthah's eye and that stern square setting to his jaw had not been softening all these days of battle. And now the Ephraimites saw it. And got it! Trapped and beaten there in the Jordan Valley, Jephthah caught them at every ford and river crossing as they tried to escape over the stream. In one of the most famous tales of military encounter ever recorded, there is still preserved the detailed account of Jephthah and his password. All those years of life as a bandit, living by wit, by cunning, by stealth —and by password—show up in this fascinating episode. As Ephraimite after Ephraimite went to his death trying to say the "Shibboleth" that a peculiarity in dialect would not allow him to pronounce properly, Jephthah the bandit was becoming the experienced warrior.

And I start to chuckle to myself, not chuckling because of the horrible death of the Ephraimites, but chuckling at a whimsy that has just struck me—for there are a lot of people today who say these stories are merely myths, not real "experiences" at all. Just how ignorant can people be.

But the chuckle dies in my throat. For I remember some-thing else. Not a myth or fable or legend. No! A vow! I am worried by a vow. That vow the so-real Jephthah made to his so little-known God. I haven't been able to forget it. As city after city falls, as every added conquest brings him nearer to victory, it also brings him nearer to home. My heart is in turmoil as mile after mile the distance lessens.

Until at last it is over, the final conquest is accomplished, it is the road back to Gilead. Until in fact it is his own home town, the watchtower town itself. Swinging along the dusty road, voices hoarse from singing and carousing, who could miss the approaching victors. Laden with every bit of Ammonite booty they can carry, Jephthah and his men are home. Jephthah has led his men on his last and greatest raid, the successful bandit is in fact the great warrior.

And I want to put my hands over my ears, to shut my eyes for ever, if only I can escape this final scene. For I have not only the vast privilege, but also the enormous responsibility, of knowing Christ, as He taught us the ultimate truth of this relationship of faith. And I remember —I can't put it out of my mind for a single second, now, it seems—the words He Himself gave us: "No man is worthy of me who cares more for son or daughter ..."

Oh, Master, I am pleading, but not Jephthah. He's never had a "home" before. This is the first chance in all his life to live in a proper home and enjoy it as a man should, with wife and child in the centre, and surrounded by the people he can at last call his own. Oh, God, please, as he comes striding up the street, as all the people come out shouting and cheering and singing in the near-delirium of victory, please let Jephthah forget that dreadful vow. And if he doesn't forget it, if he just can't forget it, then let the first person to come out of his home be some old, near-to-death retainer whose sacrifice would not hurt Jephthah further. Oh, dear God, please ...

And the cry that chokes in my very throat is lost in the great bellowing sob of agony from Jephthah. For there, throwing open the door in the excitement that is youth and the flash of bright colour that is girl, singing and dancing to the throb of the tambourine, is his daughter. His only daughter. His only child.

Do you wonder that I find this story so hard to write, so hard to comprehend? Can any man really understand the love of God?

As the young arms are thrown so warmly and passionately round Jephthah's neck, as the hot girlish kisses fall on the wet salty tears that are now pouring down the great warrior's cheeks, I feel I want to slink away and just die. If ever God was willing to let me see the depth of the wretchedness that human wickedness can evoke, surely it is in this man's life. The cruel hurt to the baby, to the boy, to the youth—this is just a trifle alongside the endless misery of the man. The burning lust that conceives a child into a start like this, the selfish hatred that drives him out of his father's home like this, worst of all the superstitious ignorance that teaches him ideas about God like this—all these are the very life of Jephthah.

Yes, I do see it. Indeed, it is because I do in fact see it, and see it so clearly, that I am so disturbed. The demand of God is always for the man himself. And if anything—anyone, even, Christ insists—comes before God in the life and emotion and attention of that man, then he cannot be one of God's men.

For this is what Jephthah has really been showing me. Not his prowess as a great warrior. Still less his skill as a bandit. Least of all the sort of knowledge he had learned in Tob about the nature of God—oh dear, no. But the stark reality of his utter obedience to the call of God, as he understood it—this he has certainly been showing me. That's why his name is among those men of faith. For faith is that unique relationship in which a man, a mere creature, sets out to serve God, and serve God alone.

The rest of the story is just as simple as it is sad. As the sob-shaken warrior told his excited daughter of his vow, of the meaning of his tears, it was she who comforted him and encouraged him. It was this same nameless daughter who insisted that the vow of faith is ultimate. It was the spiritual insight of this sub-teenager that was alert enough and clear enough to demand that the call of God must come before the love of life, even the love of the life of an only daughter.

There is a poignantly sad yet sublime account of the daughter's own personal challenge by God. She lived in a hard, tough, bitter world of constant struggle for simple survival. And to the girl of her day there was only one utter failure, and that was to be childless. In the polygamy of their society, to be unmarried was sheer unthinkable disgrace.

And now this daughter was to die, and to die childless and unwed. "Father," she said through her own tears, this time, "God has given you victory over the Ammonites, and you must keep your bargain with God. Daddy, you must. But would you allow me two months? Then I can go into the mountains with some of my new friends I have found here in Mizpah. Can I go for two months, and we will be able to talk over the things we would have planned and done and tell God all about it? I am still a virgin, and I want to go and think about it all and talk about it. And I suppose I'll cry about it too."

She was just a kid, really. We don't even know her name, or her mother's name. But I have no question in my mind that God knows her name. When the full Honours Roll of Heaven is made up, when all the saints of God are accounted for, her name will be there. It may not be in that ultra-select short list in the eleventh chapter of the Epistle to the Hebrews; but it will be in the complete roll of all the people of God.

And so she died. And so Jephthah died also, only a few short years later. And Jephthah, the bandit bastard who became the great warrior, is in fact Jephthah, the man of faith, a Son of God ...

SAMSON

Manoah's wife came dashing home absolutely bursting with her excitement and good news. You could hear her high-pitched calling away down the street even before she was in sight. "Manoah, Manoah, Man-o-o-o-ah!"

Manoah was there at the gate as she ran up, too breathless to do more than gasp, but not too breathless to blurt it all out. "Oh, Manoah! Manoah! Listen! I can't believe it. He must be a man from God. Manoah, you should have seen him—he certainly had a look on his face like a messenger from God. Oh, it was terrific. I was so upset I didn't ask where he came from. I didn't even ask him what his name was."

Manoah waited patiently. Manoah was that sort of husband. He was the waiting patiently type. His wife was getting her breath back now and she could go on again. "Manoah, he said to me, 'You are going to have a baby. A boy.' Manoah, just think, we will have a son of our own. I'm so excited. And then he said, 'You're to take no strong drink and you must keep to the strict diet of your religion. This is very important. And the boy must be brought up as a Nazirite to God, right from his birth.' And then he said to me, as serious and solemn as anything I've ever heard in all my life—he said, 'He will strike the first blow to deliver Israel from the power of the Philistines.' Those are his exact words. Just fancy, Manoah, our son will be chosen to begin our deliverance from the hated Philistines. Manoah, isn't it all *wonderful*! What shall we call him?"

And so Manoah found he was to become a father. There are many ways of making this discovery, but Manoah's was just about unique. For he had been married for a very long time now, and he and his wife were childless, and childless in a culture where that was utter poverty, total loss. They were tribespeople from the tribe of Dan, perhaps the most insignificant tribe in all Israel at that time, the tribe that didn't even have a proper bit of country of its own, and which had to live as a sort of permanent hanger-on house guest to the tribe of Judah. Devout, very devout, ultra-devout, Manoah and his unnamed wife lived in the poverty of a race that was subject to the domination and subjection of Philistine might; and in the pitiful penury of having to accept charity from another tribe. But worst of all, childless.

No wonder the poor wife was so excited. For now she would have a baby at last. Never mind the ignominy of having to share their tribal billet with Judah, mind even less the bitterness of being subject to the godless Philistines—she was to have a baby. And it was to be a boy. So at last it all came out. Manoah just waited until all her nearly hysterical outburst was quietened, and then he got it all straight. It seemed that she had met a stranger who had announced as coolly as you could wish that her prayers for a baby were heard, and she was on the maternity list at last. And I think of my obstetric colleagues, with their X-rays and salpingograms and keto-steroid estimations and all the other things I don't even remember—and this chap could do all that and more, for not only could he announce that it was to be a baby, but that it was to be a baby boy.

But she also told Manoah about the other details. They were the really important things, and she had no doubt about them. The diet, the restrictions on alcohol and any fruit from a vine, and the particular restrictions for the boy himself when he arrived. For he was never to have a razor near his head; and he was never to touch any dead body or anything that had been in touch with a dead body; and nothing from a vine, of course; and he was to be a Nazirite to God not only all his life, but even from *before* he was born.

Manoah was cautious. He was the serious, careful type. He was the sort of man who wants to get it all straight, and what's more, he's the sort of husband who wants to get it all straight from the obstetrician himself. And this tense, excitable, fluffy little wife of his didn't even get the chap's name!

And Manoah prayed. Really prayed. "Oh, God, help us. Please help us to find this man. Please send him back to us, and please may I meet him too. I do particularly want to know what I should do with our son when he is born. Please, God, help us."

Now today there is no particular mystery about a Nazirite vow. We can just look it up in the sixth chapter of the Book of Numbers, and read it in simple modern English if we are not clever enough to follow some old, out-dated text, and it's sensible enough. Moses taught his people about this vow as a special enactment to be undertaken for a special occasion. That was that.

But Manoah and his wife didn't have a nice leather-bound copy of Moses' enactments or anything like it. They were poor Danites living in penury, and no doubt most of their ideas came from memories and traditions and perhaps just the very rare privilege of actually hearing a part of the text actually read.

But God doesn't accept men or reject men because of their knowledge. God is not just the head examiner checking men off by a computerised theological pass list. Of course not. God judges men by their deliberate obedience to the things that they do know. And Manoah may have been pretty vague in the matter of some of his information, but he was truly a man of obedience. And the obedience that is faith is expressed in the prayer of faith.

And God heard his prayer.

It was Mrs. Manoah who met the visitor again. I'm human enough to think that she was so excited that she just kept both eyes wide open for any glimpse of him—the one who is truly seeking is the one who will find. And Manoah's wife was truly united with her husband in his prayer—she was truly seeking too. And I am clinician enough to think that the man himself was interested enough to be keenly on the look-out for her!

There she was, working out in the fields, when he

appeared. Manoah was not with her, but with a quick, "Wait!
I'll be right back", and a flashing of skirts she was gone.

"Manoah! Manoah! Mano-o-o-ah!" This time Manoah
came sprinting out the door to meet her. "Quick!" she
panted, "come on. That man is here. Come on. The man
who told me about our baby."

And I just can't help the smile that is in my mind as I
read of this encounter. For Manoah had been terribly serious
as he had prayed for this meeting; but now that it had really
happened he was not nearly so much at ease. He was certainly not the sort of man who found it easy to speak to
total strangers, especially about intimate things like having
babies. In fact I'm more than half sure that he was not the
sort of man who liked strange men talking to his wife about
it either. But this was the man, and he had to face up to the
interview.

"Er. Good morning. You are the man who er—spoke to
this lady?"

The stranger didn't help him much. "Yes," he said, "I
am."

"Well then," Manoah went on awkwardly, "when it happens, what you told her? What about the boy? That's what
I want to know. What must I do? What is the way he should
be brought up?"

And so they went over it all again. The restrictions on
the eating and drinking of the expectant mother, the details
that had already been explained to her in full. I know
exactly how the stranger must have felt, every doctor does,
as time and time again we are asked to repeat to spouse or
parent or other relative what we have just said in full detail
to the patient.

But this time Manoah had it all too, and now that he had
it direct he was at ease. "Well, thank you very much. I do
appreciate all you have told me. And we would certainly
like you to join us in a meal, I'll go and get a kid prepared
for roasting, and we do hope you can stay and be our guest."

The stranger looked keenly at Manoah. "If you insist on
my staying, I will do so. But if you prepare a meal for me,

please prepare it as an offering to God."

Manoah was just a little puzzled. Much of this over-serious, over-devout behaviour of people like Manoah is really just superstition, the superstition that regards some parts of life as being more sacred than others, the idea that God is more involved in the solemn and the religious than He is in the light-hearted and the mundane.

There was a moment's hesitation. Then the words just blurted themselves out. "Sir, what is your name? We would like to know who you are, so that when all you have told us has happened we can honour you properly for it."

I think the stranger smiled. In their culture, asking a man what his name was is much like asking a man today to call you by your Christian name. It was a mark of quite real familiarity, something never to be presumed or regarded as cheap. But his visitor's smile was warm, and dispelled any thought of open rebuke. "Why do you need to know my name? Why not think of it as a name to wonder at?"

So the kid was dressed, the fire was set, the flames applied, and the whole meal became an offering to God, a thank-offering to God Who works wonders. And I think there were tears in the eyes of Manoah and his wife, as they stood there arm in arm, watching the leaping flames and the spitting fat as it burst into pungent smoke: tears of joy and happiness that were indeed tears of wonderment. For it was to be a boy.

And he was gone. The stranger had gone. In the leaping flames and billowing smoke he had disappeared! Vanished!

Manoah was on his face, now, and so was his wife. The joy and the elation were wiped clean off the man's now fear-whitened face as he turned to his wife. "Oh!" he gasped, "that was God. That man was a divine messenger. Now we will die! We have seen God!"

But the practicality that is woman overlooked the logic of superstition. "Nonsense!" she burst out. "Of course God doesn't want to kill us. If He had wanted to kill us He wouldn't have bothered to accept an offering from us or go to all this bother about us, or to tell us all the things He has shown us."

No, God had not wanted to kill them, of course not. God wanted them to have a son. And they called him Samson.

Now if you are suggesting, as well you might be, that all this long preamble to the story of Samson is tedious and quite unexciting, then let me assure you that I am more than sympathetic. These simple people, with their unthinking piety and over-serious religiosity can be ponderous company, to be sure, and there are many people who find it all rather cloying. Yes, I understand. But if this is heavy, ponderous, slow-moving reading matter, then you may imagine the effect it is all going to have on the boy who simply exploded into its very midst.

For that is the home background of this, the most colourful of all personalities in the whole Bible. David and his sling and stone, Daniel and his den of lions, Jonah and his whale, even Esther and the king of Persia—none of these can compare with the sheer full-blooded dynamic of Samson.

And unless we can grasp the pathos and the conflict that a background like this must inevitably make in a lad like this, a lad all muscle and movement and mirth, then we will never grasp how or why Samson's name is in that élite list of men of faith in Hebrews, chapter eleven. Look at it as a bit of T.V. adventure story, and it's nearly fairytale; see it as the romantic entanglement of a highly susceptible youth from the outback, and it's tawdry. (And even some of the preachers themselves, the convention and holiness meeting pundits in particular, see it as an example of the undisciplined extravagance of an immature prankster who frittered away his true potential. Yes, I have actually heard and read nonsense like that.)

But see it as the great surging drama of the repressed, tense mother and the serious, bewildered father into whose ageing lives has burst this bundle of hormone-packed boy —and you're on your way to an insight into one of the most heart-stirring, poignantly human accounts ever recorded in literature. And recorded by none other than God Himself.

And then, and then only, you may realise why Samson's name is in the Honour Roll of Heaven.

"The boy grew up in Mahaneh-dan between Zorah and Eshtaol, and the Lord blessed him, and the spirit of the Lord began to drive him hard." That is what the old historian says. That is all the old historian says. The whole of that boyhood and youth is summed up in those twenty-six words. There are a thousand questions any parent would like to ask about that kid and his home, and another thousand any child might like to ask: yet twenty-six words are all you find to get your answers from.

Questions? My goodness there are questions. For that boy is not just an only child, and that may be difficult enough; but he is a bit of a freak. You can pick him out just walking down the street—he's got long hair where all the other boys' hair is short. At the birthday parties and the festival seasons he doesn't eat grapes or raisins or drink any wine when all the other lads do. When the kids are out playing together and somebody finds a dead frog or a dead lizard or any such other of the thousand treasures that boys love to find—Samson isn't allowed to touch it, he's a Nazirite. And when his uncle died, and then his grandmother, he couldn't go near the coffin for a last look—he had to stay and watch through blinding tears from the heart-breaking distance that all this awkward religion demanded.

Sure, Samson grew up, and that's how he did it. And the other kids couldn't tease him or crack jokes about him or poke fun at him—not Samson. Why, that boy could just pick up the biggest lad in the whole village and toss him clean across the pavement in one heave. And do it with one hand! No, no teasing and jossing and taunting when Samson was about, with his long hair and strange customs and funny religious ideas. No, you'd better be careful, jolly careful, see, Samson is growing up.

Of course God doesn't bother to record all these details, as the boy grew up. Can't we recognise the pressure and turmoil of his boyhood in the reactions and qualities that erupt in adult life? Of course!

But "the boy grew ... and the Lord blessed him". The growing-up bit is straightforward enough, it's just the way with boys, and what is seen in later life is so very much the product of this growing-up process—if it were just "left to nature". But God doesn't just "leave it to nature". God is moving into this boy's growing-up experience to bless him, and that is going to make all the difference in the world, and all the difference in Heaven, in what goes on. For Samson, boy-becoming-man, is one of God's men of faith, he is in fact to be a Son of God, if he but knew it. And I wonder how much Samson ever guessed that the Lord blessed him, as his broad shoulders began to jostle against the narrow confines of his so-zealous father's and mother's world, as his Olympian speed chafed against the slow-running caution of his ultra-conservative home. Yes, the Lord was starting to bless him; but how much of it felt like blessing to the boy himself? That is indeed the question.

But there is something else: "the Spirit of God began to drive him hard". That is something I don't remember reading anywhere else in the whole Bible. Yet it is something that is in fact happening in the lives of countless youngsters in all history. God is working on that boy, God is talking with that girl—the Spirit of God is driving them! For it was Jesus who told us that when God's Spirit comes into human affairs, He "will show where wrong and right and judgment lie". And that's certainly a driving enough experience in the most uncomplicated life that any simple man ever lived. But in a so utterly out-of-place setting like Samson in the home of Manoah, then watch out! Something will have to give way.

That "the boy grew" I can take for granted. That "the Lord blessed him" I can accept readily enough, even though it may be more than baffling time and time again.

But when the Spirit of God begins to drive him hard then I may well bow in awe: for God is now engaged in the Heaven-sized wonder of transforming a human, a mere biologically evolved animal, into a Son of God. And that is what the story of Samson is really all about . . .

Samson was in love. Infatuated. Really smitten. He was barely middle-to-late teens, but his long, flowing hair and his now quite respectable beard topping a torso of unparalleled muscular excellence made him a remarkable figure of young manhood. And backed now by the driving passions of adult male hormones, no wonder Samson was in love.

Samson was sitting with his chair tilted on its back legs, boots (mud and all) on the mantelpiece, his hands folded behind his head, his gaze fixed firmly on a knot-hole in one of the rafters straight above him. He did not move or shift his eyes as he spoke—Samson was a teenager.

"Hey, dad! Listen, mum! I've got a girl. She's terrific. I want to marry her. Will you go and get her for me? I want her." Samson's requests were in the nature of commands—at home.

Dad looked up rather timidly and mum's face was just pink with the slight blush of excitement. I have no doubt at all that for months and months now they had been checking and re-checking on every single girl in all their tribe of Dan; there wasn't one feminine dossier they didn't know down to the last ringlet and dimple. But this surprised them. Caught them quite unawares.

Dad's mouth began to open, he got as far as clearing his throat slightly; but it was mum who asked the question. "Who is it, Samson? Who is the girl?"

"Girl down in Timnah. She's a Philistine girl and she's terrific. I want to marry her. You get her for me as my wife."

I must confess that I still feel a slightly leaden heaviness deep within me every time I think of this little scene. This precious boy, now so nearly a man, in whom all their hopes and prayers are centred, suddenly blurting out this shocking, dreadful, unbelievable blasphemy. A Philistine. A girl from Timnah. Not just another creed, another race or colour, not merely a matter of human and cultural differences like that. Not just a religious problem like a catholic falling in love with a protestant. Not even a social calamity such as a scion of Old Boston falling in love with a Negress. No! This was linking light with darkness. It was demanding a liaison between God and mammon!

What a scene! Samson still gazing at the knot-hole, feet unmoved from the mantelpiece, pretending a nonchalance and casualness that he certainly did not feel. He knew the storm would burst, but he was used to that now, it would pass and he would get his way. He always did. Mum would blow a fuse completely, dad would mumble and fumble and finish up thoroughly hard to get on with, but the boy would always win.

"Oh, Samson, that's terrible!" And mother dissolved into a flood of hot, sniffling, face-dabbing tears.

Dad was slower finding words, but they were more meaningful words. "You can't do it, Samson. Not a girl from the godless Philistines. That's a most terribly wicked thing even to think about. Why can't you find a wife among your own kinsfolk? Or even in some other part of your own nation, if you like? But fancy thinking of a Philistine. I'll have nothing to do with her, and I can tell you that straight." And dad sat back bolt upright in righteous indignation and began to mutter to himself. It was the sort of muttering that was really a quite recognisable mumble, and they could all hear that it was the parts he could remember relating to the vows of the Nazirite. And in this pretence he dismissed the whole sordid unpleasantness with a final deep growl.

But not mother. Mother's tears were still pouring freely, though her voice was recovering. Yet the words and the sniffles and the sobs were all so mixed that it was hard to pick up more than the general gist of it. "Ohhh, Samson! A Philistine girl. A Philistine daughter-in-law. All our neighbours will cut us dead. I'd never be able to go shopping in the village ever again—my only daughter-in-law a Philistine. Oh, Samson, the shame of it would kill me!" And now she put her head down in her hands and sobbed loudly and piteously and endlessly.

Poor Manoah. Poor wife. They don't really know it, of course, but the Spirit of God is driving them, too. God is

using this tragedy (and it is certainly nothing short of tragedy
to them, the serious old dears) to "drive" them, really to
perfect them. Their zeal, their fervour, their reputation for
punctilious scruple in every detail of their cult—all this is
challenged. Yes, the "blessing" of God is often very difficult
to understand, but when the Spirit of God drives hard in
human experience then the very depths of our being are
exposed. But this is not the story of Manoah and his wife;
this is not recorded just to show us how God challenges
even our religion, asking always, "Do you love Me? Am I
first in your heart? Do I always come ahead of rite and
ceremony and creed and liturgy and dogma? Do you serve
Me with all your heart? And all your mind? And all your
strength?"

No, this is Samson's story. And Samson certainly doesn't
know it, as he sits back in his chair, muddy boots still on
the mantelpiece, hands clasped behind his head, eyes still
fixed on that so-convenient knot-hole. No, Samson hasn't
a clue in the world as to what is really happening. He thinks
it's a matter of a smashing good sort of a lass he's found
down in Timnah, a matter of a couple of real stuffy fuddy-
duddies in the persons of a mum and dad who haven't woken
up to the fact that this is a new age altogether and the kids
aren't like they were in your time and things just keep
moving fast and it's now the late twentieth century and
science has taught us how all these old religious shibboleths
are terribly outmoded and it's really bad for a fellow to be
restricted by these old-fashioned customs and God is really
not what our grandmothers used to think back in those fusty
Victorian days and ... I'm sorry, Samson, I'm so used to
the kids I meet every day in my own modern Sydney that
I forgot for a moment that you are three thousand years away.
But, Samson, I think I do understand pretty well what is
bothering the teenagers of my own world, and my sympathy
and my concern is with them; and I know that while your
physique may be finer than any single youth in Australia
today (and that includes a whole stack of world champion
swimmers and surfers and athletes and tennis players and

golfers and almost anything else you care to name) and your hormones are churning you up to an ecstasy of passion— Samson, you're still made of the same basic material as are our fellows today, and I think I do indeed understand you pretty well.

But, Samson, whether I understand you all pretty well or not isn't very important; that is only a matter of a bit of advice and a prescription or two: what matters is that God understands you entirely. He knows every single molecule in your whole biochemistry. It is in fact the Spirit of God Who is driving you so hard.

Yes, Samson, that is what is utterly important. But if you really want to get your own way, then my advice to you (take it or leave it) would be to sit absolutely pat and don't budge an inch. You've found the girl you like—you don't as yet know at all that God is now driving you—just dig your toes in and tell mum and dad to quit all the blabbing and fussing and go and get the girl and line up the wedding and that's what you want and that's what you're going to have, see, and if they don't do it properly then you can't see why you shouldn't just take the girl and live with her and be hanged to all these middle-class restrictions. So just get cracking, mum and dad, and start to grow up. And you'll like her no end when you see her, mum, she's the cutest kid you ever met. And you'll find the Philistines a lot of good fun, if you only got to know them, dad, and you'll have the best holiday in all your life and you'll only be sorry it's not your own honeymoon you're planning all over again.

Sure, Samson, the strength that comes to your poor old parents from a mere set of rules, from just keeping up with a code, is not very great strength at all. And you know that. You have found that out a thousand times already, and as you simply sit back staring at that knot-hole in the rafter over your head you know you'll win. The old couple can't beat you, not when they are strengthened by such feeble support.

But I must in all fairness add this, Samson: it won't be

many weeks now before mum and dad know that too. For as you all go down to Timnah (yes, you'll win, as you always have won so far) your dear old parents are going to learn what it is to put their whole trust in God and not merely rely in the Nazirite code. And you, Samson, are being driven on by the wonder of the love of God as He begins to teach you the very same thing; you are on the way to learning not to put your trust in your strength or your passions or your Philistine friends or your Philistine girl friends any more than in the Nazirite vows you so thoroughly despise. Samson, you are going to have to trust in God, and in God alone. Samson, the Spirit of God is beginning to drive you, drive you and drive you and drive you until you become completely re-created into a Son of God. Samson, hurrah for Timnah and that faithless little Philistine beauty who has captured your so-vulnerable heart—the Spirit of God is driving you. And He is using her (the little devil!) as His driving agent.

There were vineyards in Timnah, it was wine country. Rich, sweet, juicy grapes for making the smoothest, headiest, most fragrant of wines. Philistine country, wine country.

And I blink, and rub my eyes, and blink again—has something gone wrong with my eyes, am I so old that I'm not seeing too well as I gaze across the vineyard? But that looks like Samson, the long-haired bearded Nazirite, out there in the vineyard. His parents are down in the village, negotiating the dowry and the wedding arrangements with the bride's parents. But can this possibly be Samson out here in the very centre of the forbidden grapes?

Yes. It is Samson ... Samson among the grapes. Samson, being driven hard by the Spirit of God.

And Samson is not alone. I can see a slight movement among the vines. I can't quite see who it is—is it his bride-to-be, coming to meet him in the shady secrecy of the sheltering branches? But no, it's not quite like that, I wish I had my binoculars, it's just a vague shadowy movement, it's—*Samson!*

The cry that bursts from me is still far too late to warn

him. For it's a lion! Samson has come upon a young lion,
out there in the Philistine vineyard.

But it's all too quick to see even if I had binoculars and
telephoto lens and slow-motion camera and all. For even as
the lion springs, Samson springs too. And in a sudden flurry
of convulsive movement it is over. Up in the air flails the
carcass of the lion, torn clean in half by the might and the
speed of Samson's two bare hands. And as the dead body
comes thudding to the earth, blood and entrails gushing from
its bifurcated body, Samson just turns on his heel and strides
off. Not even a backward glance, just strides off to Timnah
to find out how the wedding arrangements are going on.
Not a word to anybody about the vineyard and the lion.
Certainly not to mum and dad, not even to his little Philistine sweetheart when he goes to meet her again for a while.
No, nothing about the vineyard or the lion, not to her.

And so the preparations got under way. A Philistine wedding was then (as weddings are now) quite a ceremony. In
fact even more then than now. A modern wedding takes
nearly half a day—theirs took a whole week. But Timnah
was not very far from Zorah, and Samson could easily make
the trip in an hour. And so could mum and dad, now that
they were properly involved in the whole thing.

So the weeks of planning passed, and Samson and his
parents came back to Timnah for the ceremony. Samson is
to marry the godless Philistine beauty he has picked out for
himself. And one day Samson paid another visit to the vineyard where he had killed the young lion. And there, in the
carcass of the dead beast, was a swarm of bees and already
a mass of honeycomb. Of course a Nazirite would never go
near a dead body of any sort, and honey from such a hiding-
place would be utterly and absolutely abhorrent. But Samson
now really considered himself a Philistine. He was a man,
sure enough he was; he had lately ripped a lion in half;
he was marrying a delightful Philistine girl; and while his
long hair and flowing beard made him look like a Nazirite,
at heart he was sure he was much too grown-up for all that

childish stuff, and his sweetheart thought his long hair looked cute and he thought it did rather suit him, sure it did, and even the Philistine boys looked at him in something that was almost envy as much as it was awe—my, but the honey tasted good, as he scraped it out of the lion's body with his bare hands. Yes, and why not give a bit to mum and dad? They'd feel sick if they knew it came out of a dead body, especially a dead lion's body—lions are "unclean" even when alive—but they needn't know, the dears. Just tell them I found it in the trees when I was out for a walk, and if they don't know about it they won't be upset by it, they'll even enjoy it.

And mother said what a sweet, thoughtful, loving boy, it was beautiful honey. And dad said yes, considering it came from Philistine country it was surprisingly good, and thanks, son, we hope we can see you happy, that's all we are really trying to do.

Samson: the Spirit of God is continuing to drive you, and that lion and that honey are really part of the strange machinery that God will use in the endless patience and skill with which He re-creates a mere human into a divine Son.

At last it's time for the wedding. Samson is to marry the Timnite beauty, God is to be united with Mammon. This should be quite an event!

Yes, it was quite an event!

Manoah licked the final taste of honey from his lips and now his big day had arrived. His job was to go to the bride's home and organise a feast for the groom. And I think dad was rather stunned and even Samson was just a bit dismayed when the locals literally came to the party to the tune of no less than thirty groomsmen. That's what I said—thirty groomsmen. One was appointed best man and the others made a highly impressive string of off-siders. I must confess that I just don't entirely understand their motivation in rallying round in such numbers. Was it because Samson had found a place of such warm and spontaneous affection in their hearts? No! I don't think that. I don't think the

hostile world around ever really takes a man of God to its
heart, even if the man of God is apparently indistinguish-
able at first glance from any other of the labourers out feeding the pigs. No, I don't think that.

I think they turned up in such numbers because of fear
and bitterness. The fear that always fills Philistines when
they take a man of God into their ranks—and there is
strength in numbers. And the bitterness that they felt because
this uncouth bounder could come and captivate one of their
charming little birds—and this way they could make him
pay for it, the blighter.

Yes, that's what I think, and that's pretty much what
Samson thought as he saw this thirty-long string of groomsmen. For Samson knew something else: he knew that he
was supposed to outfit each of them in a suit of festal garments. Yes, he had to foot that thirty-man tailor's bill! And
as he saw the half-hidden smirks and heard the half-whispered jokes and felt the half-concealed sneers, Samson had
no questions left. These men weren't mates. Not a real
dinkum pal among the lot of them. Philistines, that's what
they were, just Philistines.

Now then, Samson, you're learning a lot of things this
morning, and learning them fast: but at least you've learned
that Philistines don't waste any time and effort on genuine
brotherly affection and unqualified generosity and open
altruism—not Philistines. Come on, Samson, thirty tailored
outfits, several years' total income, and here's the bill.

And Samson's face whitened a short moment, and then
flushed slightly. The combined taunt and challenge couldn't
be passed over—in a flash he had his answer. "OK, fellows,
thanks for coming. Drinks all round, waiter, and it's on me.
Here's to a merry good time."

And as the elbows went up and the drinks went down,
the glasses all clanked to a noisy emptiness. "Listen, you
chaps. How would you like to take a little bet? Good sporting risk, you people are great sportsmen, we hear. Like to
take a wager?"

Thirty Philistine faces began to light up. This cheap bum

from the scrubland is going to be more fun than we had
even hoped. First he's stung for the price of the wedding
garments, and now here he is running a stake-game with
us. Boy, oh boy, what a lovely big sucker this drip is!

"Well, then, here is my wager. I'll put up a riddle, and if
you can give me the answer before this feast is over, then
I'll stand each of you a brand-new linen outfit, as well as
all the wedding trimmings. And if you can't answer my
riddle, then you owe me thirty suits. A sort of double or
quits. How's that?"

Now to us that sounds crazy, it's a game we have never
played. But they had never heard of poker or two-up either,
yet this scheme of Samson's was in fact one they did know
about. And they nodded their ready agreement. "OK, Samson, tell us your riddle. We'll take your bet."

And Samson put his riddle:

> *"Out of the eater came something to eat,*
> *Out of the strong came something sweet."*

And I want to burst into cheering, not because it was
such a teaser of a riddle, but because I could recognise—
how could I fail to recognise—why, this is the Spirit of
God beginning to drive Samson with the lion and the honey.
You Philistines, I wanted to blurt out, you'd better be careful. Jolly careful indeed! This is not Samson you're betting
against, it's the Spirit of God. You'd be wise to call it right
off and pay up now.

But the Philistines wouldn't have heard me, even if I had
blurted it out. For they were in a little huddle, trying to
work out the answer. "Eater? ... Something to eat? ..."
"Strong? ... Something sweet? ..." "*Out* of the eater ...
out of the strong ..." "The *eater* ... the *strong* ..."

Shades of all the crossword puzzles in history. Round and
round and back and forth went the words and the couplet
and the guesses and the ideas. Thirty heads and thirty
tongues now with only one single thought and one single
question. All day. All the next day. All the day after that.

Three days gone, half the time of the feast was now over, and no answer to the riddle. And the hot roasts and the sweet side-dishes and the hors d'œuvres and the cheeses all came and all went, and the smooth, heady, fragrant wines did nothing to help. No solution. Not a clue. No answer.

And the feast was now into its fourth day and they were thirty angry, worried, unhappy groomsmen indeed. Nice party, thank you!

It was the new wife, the little Timnite, Mrs. Samson, that they approached. "Listen, Gertie, and listen carefully. That big lout of a husband of yours has us all loused up with a stupid riddle that just doesn't make one word of sense. It's the most unsporting riddle we've ever met up with, and you can quote us on that. Only an absolutely impossible cad of a no-hope bounder would even think of such a dirty bit of play. Now you find out what that riddle means, and find out for sure. We don't care how you do it, but just come back with that answer! You get to work on him and wheedle it out of him by hook or by crook. Take our advice, Tootsie darling, and get it. It'd be a pity if we had to burn you up with your old father, wouldn't it? We don't think your old man likes getting burned, really. Don't you agree? OK, sweetheart, get to work on that big slob of a husband of yours."

Of course by this time the whole wedding party was caught up in it. Samson, beginning to feel pretty smug, the thirty Philistine groomsmen beginning to look like black fury, the general run of guests and hangers-on and by-standers all beginning to titter and lay side-wagers on the wager. *Very* nice party, thank you. Going with a real bang.

And the little bride beginning to look sad. As she cuddled up to Samson so sweetly, her dainty cheeks were faintly tear-stained, her cherry lips puckered into a pout, nobody could fail to see that the bride was unhappy. Even doting Samson got the message. "What's the matter, my sweet little chick? You don't look happy. What is it?"

She pushed his arms from their embrace and moved away from him. "You don't love me at all. You really hate me.

You don't love me a bit." And she dabbed at the tears that ought to have been there in her eyes and tossed back her head as she stamped her foot on the ground.

"Aw, darling, you know I love you. Of course I do. What on earth gives you those silly ideas? You must be tired, it's all this long party, you'll be all right when we're away on our own."

"No! You do really hate me. You don't love me a single bit. You've put a riddle to all my friends and you haven't even told me the answer. You just hate me!" And she buried her head in her hands and sobbed loudly and passionately.

"Listen, sweetie, but I haven't even told it to my mother and father. It's a riddle; they've got to work it out. It wouldn't be a riddle if I went round telling people the answer. Now don't be silly. Come and enjoy the party and let these fellows work it out."

Hmmm ... Samson—and here I am smiling a wry smile —you're a great big boy and no end of a singles player in the great Wimbledon of life, but right down here in Philistine country you're a regular babe in the wood. You've grown up in a game you've played all your young life with mum and dad, and they absolutely dote on you. That cross-court of yours to the forehand, they never really tried to get back into play; that lollypop smash you put up at the net, they didn't really try to kill—no, Samson, they have hardly played against you ever, you don't know what a thoroughly tough game this little old world can turn on for a fellow. But now you're learning. Learning fast, too, you'll find. That captivating Philistine who's supposed to be playing with you— she's a drop-out, Samson! She's not serving to win for you —she's going to double-fault every time. She'll toss the game away and never bat an eyelid. Samson, she's a Philistine and she's only ever learned to play the game the way Philistines play it.

Yes, Samson was learning. The week wasn't even over before he found out. As his sobbing and resisting and altogether rejecting wife cajoled and tormented and finally ensnared him, out poured the secret. The riddle of the lion and the honey and the forbidden vineyard. I think Samson genuinely thought that now it was the very last day of the festival, now that it was nearly sunset and only an hour or so remaining in which she had to keep her mouth shut and preserve his secret, why, he was safe enough, surely. Even the most tittle-tattle wife in the world could hardly tell a secret in that short time.

Ha! Ha! Ha! And now I burst out in harsh, raucous laughter. Samson, you thick-skulled, addle-pated nitwit! Of all the absolute numskulls in the cut and thrust of life, you get the number one rating. Samson, it's only half an hour since you told her your secret, she's only left you for a single minute to pay a visit to the powder-room—and listen, Samson, they're coming now. Can't you hear them? Can you take your infatuated mind off your lying, cheating, two-timing little Philistine heart-throb for just a single moment and wake right up? Snap out of it, Samson, they're here! Standing right beside you, oaf, smirking and sneering and mocking you openly.

"Say, Samson." It was the leader of the group, the fellow who was his best man. "Samson, we nearly forgot, but luckily just remembered before sunset. That riddle. You remember your riddle? Good, you *do* remember it. Well, what do you think of this?"

> *"What is sweeter than honey?*
> *What is stronger than a lion?"*

I thought Samson would collapse, just for the first moment. If they had ligated both carotid arteries, if they had wired him to a Wimshurst machine, if they had doused him with a bucket of liquid air, the effect could hardly have been more cruel.

His face went instantly and completely grey—my first impression was a total heart block. He had his wife's right hand in his left, his right arm was round her waist, he had been gazing straight into her eyes, as the best man began to speak. And I could see that it was now really she who kept him from actually falling on his face on the floor.

And then as the colour returned, as some blood vessels filled ahead of others, as that ghastly blotchy pallor flushed first pink, then finally full-blaze fire, the heat and pent-up passion was frightening. I slipped behind a stout pillar supporting the roof-gallery, several of the Philistines darted for cover like foxes at the bay of the hound.

But there was something almost indifferent, quite unexpectedly disciplined, as speech came to him. "If you had not ploughed with my heifer, you would not have found out my riddle."

And he was gone. Not another word. He didn't even glance at them. With a mere gesture of movement he brushed his new-wed wife aside as if she were a fleck of dust that had blown in upon him with some passing squall, and he swept his way through the now cowering circle of attendants and strode out the door in sheer uncontrollable passion. Out down the road, through the town on to the highway, away into the early dusk, running at last, racing effortlessly and inexhaustibly over hill and dale, mountain and valley, far away to the south-west, clean down to the coast itself, to Askelon. No pause for rest or reflection, twenty-three non-stop miles he had covered since sundown.

And Askelon paid the price. Askelon, one of the big Philistine cities where these sea people had in fact made their first conquest. Askelon was his goal. And I am certain that never to the end of all its history could anybody from Askelon ever say for certain just what hit the town that night. Samson, it was, who hit the town. Samson, driven hard by the Spirit of God. Caught, slain outright in instant, merciless death, stripped and tossed aside in nakedness, man after man after man was taken. Until there stood Samson, flushed, excited, furious. Thirty Philistine suits of clothes now draped in lavish luxury over arms and neck and shoulders ...

Timnah was wine country. Smooth, heady, fragrant wines, in Timnah. But morning comes slowly and wearily and painfully in the land of the vintner, and Timnah was no exception. So that it was certainly long after the breakfast hour,

you could really say it was even too late for brunch, when
the festal party began to stir. Manoah and his wife had gone
home the night before, heart-broken, disillusioned, in the
abject misery of self-pity and resentment, home to hide,
home at last to pray. Yes, Manoah and his wife had gone.

But the bride was still there. She was awake, wide awake,
but she was still not up and about. She was too bewildered
to know quite what to do. Was this Samson husband ever
likely to come back? Would she ever want him back? Of
course there were the wedding presents, too. Should she
keep them, should she send them back and regard the whole
episode as a mere dream that has passed? And the best man
is a very attractive fellow, she admitted to herself so readily,
she couldn't help noticing the way he had looked at her all
through that week. Very attractive! No, the bride was not
about.

But the bride's parents were up. They had to be up,
because the guests were beginning to stir and they had to
be around to receive the formal goodbyes and rather subdued thanks of any who had to leave early.

Until at last the guests were really astir. The yawns and
the blurred focus of the morning after, the call for the hair
of the dog that bit them, the usual slightly brittle uneasiness
that marks the end of all such Philistine merry-making. But
thank goodness it's Timnah, wine country, there is still
plenty of grog. Yes, thanks, mine's another brandy. What's
yours?

But it must be Samson! Striding up the road, completely
hidden under a vast mountain of gaudy, rich Philistine
clothing, there could be no way of seeing face or form or
figure—but that dusty, sweat-stained traveller, swinging
along at such pace, could only ever be Samson. No knock
on the door—his arms completely occupied with holding
the thirty suits of clothes, no hope of knocking, even if he
had wanted—straight into the centre of the ballroom where
all the week's festivities had been held, now tossing the suits
in an enormous heap on to the dust and the scraps on the
unswept floor—there stood Samson!

Then spinning on his heel, he was gone. Not a word. Not even a grunt. Just the inexpressible fury of a night of rage and murder and hatred.

Samson went home.

It's the time of the harvest. The wheat is ripe and full in the grain and the time for reaping has come round. Harvest time in Timnah. And—bless my soul—it's Samson! Samson, strolling down the road to Timnah, Samson back in Philistine country, back in the town of his wedding. Well, what do you know? He's got a basket in his hand, I wonder what on earth it is. Say, Samson, lovely day, isn't it? What's in the basket? Picnic lunch?

Samson's answer is as much a grin as it is words. "Well, you've pretty nearly hit the mark. It's a dressed lamb, I've specially fattened it. Should taste terrific. It's for my wife. I think she'll like it." And there was now no mistaking the sparkle in his eye and the jauntiness of his step. Samson is going courting. Going to court his Philistine wife!

And now he's ringing the front door bell. Long, confident, unrestrained tugging on the bell-rope, the young swain is here to make love to his wife. Come and watch this, this should be something really worth seeing. Even Shakespeare didn't tangle with a bit of drama like this.

Dad himself answered the door bell. The Timnite girl's father. As he threw back the door and saw Samson I saw his face go white, I saw the tremble of his hand as he clutched the door for support. I'm sure the old chap had landed the job of sorting out those thirty suits of clothes in the middle of the ballroom floor the day after Samson's wedding. I am equally sure he had seen the few spattered drops of blood, I am more than sure he had guessed perfectly clearly how they had got there. And now here was Samson.

But before he could move or even open his mouth to say a word, Samson was speaking. "Good morning. Glorious day, isn't it? I've brought a little gift for my wife. I'll take it straight in, I know where her room is. I'll go and wake her up."

Father's trembling increased noticeably, he had difficulty freeing his hand from the door enough to let him mop his now fast-moistening brow. He licked his dry lips and just blurted out his objection. "No! You can't do that. You just can't do that."

Samson stood stock still and stared hard and long, straight at the older man. Any experienced clinician would recognise immediately that the nonchalant breeziness with which Samson had bowled up to the front door was in fact a mere assumption of ease. He was tensed, and Samson tense was likely to be Trouble, capital T! His Timnite father-in-law knew this. Words failed him.

But not Samson. "Yes? Why not? Why can't I do that? She's my wife, isn't she? Tell me why I can't go and see her just any time I like? Who's going to stop me? Eh?"

The Philistine was looking (and must certainly have been feeling) absolutely wretched. "B..b..but I thought you hated her. I..I..I..I ... thought you didn't like her. Oh, dear! I just supposed it was all off between you two, and ... and ... and I thought you might prefer her little sister. She's very pretty, much prettier, you know. Hers is the third door on the left down the hall. Wouldn't you like her?"

Samson didn't actually touch the older man. I really think that if he had even laid a hand on his shoulder, it would have been over—that old Philistine would have gone the way of that young lion in the vineyard—just torn to bits. But the barely restrained rage was unmistakable now. His eyes were mere slits, his lips hardly moved, the words were slow, they were hissed, not spoken. "Listen, Philistine, where is my wife?"

Samson's face was now about twelve inches from the other, his broad young shoulders seemed almost to be enveloping the wretched father-in-law. The answer seemed to be squeezed out of the old fellow. "She's with the best man. He liked her and I thought you really hated her, so I gave her to the best man. B..b..b..but her little sister is here, look, here she comes now. She's a very pretty girl, why not take her instead?"

There were now faces in the hall, at the doors, quite a little household crowd collecting up. I could see the sudden and total change in mood in Samson as he caught sight of her, as he cast a look of sheer contempt at the somewhat dishevelled younger sister who had come right into the middle of the room. She had heard her father's last few words, and I could see that she was quite excited by it all. Yes, I thought, she is pretty, quite pretty-pretty, really, not so much of the more sultry self-conscious beauty of Samson's original heart-throb.

That's what I thought, and I could realise that her dad thought that too, thought it quite genuinely.

But Samson stepped back and snapped to an almost military attention. "All right!" The word was just barked out. "You asked for it. You dirty Philistines play it like that, then you'll get it back like that. Since this is the way you want it, this is the way you'll get it, and don't ever come whining and wingeing back to tell me you want to change it. You made the rules and I'll stick to your stinking rules."

And he flashed out the door as he slammed it with a thud that rattled every single piece of bric-à-brac and ornament on all the walls in the house.

Nobody followed him. The sheer terror he had left in the emotions of that Philistine household would keep them locked behind that door for hours and hours, I could guarantee, and Samson strode off like an Olympic walker.

The dressed kid in the basket, the present he had brought for his young wife, he just tossed into some bushes beside the mountain track he was now following. I had no hope of keeping pace with him. Up, up, faster, it seemed, as it got steeper, I was left panting and puffing and blowing a long, long, way behind. I didn't know where he was going, I couldn't possibly guess what he had in mind, but I knew it was no mere guess that told me he did have something in mind. Something that was going to make trouble. Lots of trouble. Samson-sized trouble.

It was two days later that I just stumbled across him. It was up in a lonely, deserted bit of hillside, that I saw him.

In fact it is hardly correct to say I saw him or stumbled across him. It was up in a lonely, deserted bit of hillside that first my ears, then my nostrils, and last of all my eyes led me stumbling to his companions. Jackals! Dozens of jackals. Hundreds, it seemed. A sight and a sound—and a stench—that could never be missed. It was the barking—and then the stench—that brought me to the spot. The jackals had been herded into a few little caves that he had blocked off with stones, and even as I came up to investigate this unbelievable noise and smell, Samson came running up.

Now we have foxes in Australia. Only foxes. Plenty of foxes, thank you. Some of our kind, thoughtful early settlers, thinking of the gracious pleasure of the good old English hunt, brought them here. And turned them loose in the 2,000,000,000 acres of Australia. Yes, we have foxes.

But only foxes. We haven't got jackals. Not yet, at any rate. I just hate to think what it would be like if we had to contend with jackals as well. I rather think that our sheep dogs and our cattle dogs would just chew them to pieces. Jackals are skulking, cowardly, pack-hunting little beasts, and while our graziers can't clear their wheat lands of foxes I don't think they would have any great trouble getting rid of jackals if ever we were unlucky enough to be landed with them. I think they would hunt them out and shoot them and starve them out. That's what I think they would do with jackals. Just hunt them and shoot them and starve them. But what they would never seriously think of doing would be to try and catch them alive. And not even when completely drunk would any one of them think of catching them alive by hand.

And Samson was catching jackals. Alive. Catching them alive by hand. My mouth sagged open in sheer unbelieving amazement. Have you ever even in a nightmare given a thought to catching a live, healthy, completely wild jackal? Catching it in your hands? And keeping all your ten fingers intact? And there was Samson, loping in from the hills, with two. Two live jackals to add to his little zoo.

I didn't say anything. I couldn't. Of all the astonishing

things to have happened in this old world, surely this must be as absolutely zany as any one of you could name. I'm only a city dweller, and I can't for the life of me think how a man would go about catching one. And here was Samson with two. Yes, you can guess and guess and guess, and any answer you can turn up with will be much better than mine, I assure you. I just haven't got a guess in the world as to how he did it.

About three hundred. That was the tally before he was satisfied. Three hundred yelping, leaping, barking, panting —and stinking—jackals. And now, I thought, just what on earth will he be doing with them. I knew it was something for the Philistines, something to make trouble for the Philistines, that he was planning. But what?

And then I saw.

It was harvest time, remember, the time of the wheat harvest. Some of the wheat in the rich Philistine countryside was already reaped, stacked in shocks ready for collecting and threshing. Much was still uncut. And Samson was making little torches. Simple, unelaborate, brushwood torches.

And now he was tying the torches to the jackals, but tying one torch to two jackals, tail-to-tail. Working like lightning, catching the jackals as they sprang out of the opening he allowed them from the blocked-up cave, tying a torch to the pair, and lighting it as they dashed for freedom.

Some of the torches burnt out. Some of them fell off. Some of the jackals broke loose. Some of them headed straight up into the hills. Yes. Some of them did that. But the rest didn't. Oh my, Oh my! The rest didn't. What a scene! What a holocaust! For most of them did *not* burn out, did *not* fall off, did *not* break free, did *not* head straight up into the hills.

No, most of them streaked right into the surrounding wheat fields, right into the ready-stacked sheaves. And even with a grim background of Australian bush fires and enormous grass fires that can sweep thousands of acres of countryside, this beat them all. For the valley was compact, the whole of it lay spread out just like the panorama from a low-flying Cessna.

And up it all went. How fast does a jackal run? About a thousand miles an hour, I reckon, from the way that tinderbox ignited! That whole valley just flashed into flames in a criss-crossing helter-skelter of fireworks that the wildest Guy Fawkes Day in history could not hope to equal. Whooooooosh! It seemed almost to be exploding!

And it was over. Black, derelict, dreadful. Only fire can ever do this to a countryside. A few whisps of smoke still rising from a smouldering tree or shrub, a few areas still billowing dense smoke, where the fire had caught right into the scattered olive orchards—but it was really over.

Samson was sitting resting on a rock, obviously tired nearly to exhaustion point, but with a look of sheer elation wreathing his whole face. There was much I would like to ask, a few things I felt I would like to say. I would love to know how he caught those jackals—yes, I would dearly love to know that. But I would even more dearly love to ask him about the driving of the Spirit of God—did he know about that? That was the thing I would so much like to tell him about, if he did not in fact know it. Tell him that he is in truth one of God's own men, that all this tragedy and excitement and conflict and drama is really God driving him, God teaching him to love his God with all his being. To love God, strength, passion, hormones and all. Tell him most of all that God is actually remaking him, re-creating him; in the most real (though mystic) sense God is having him reborn into the very life of God, such is the love of God.

But I didn't say anything and I really didn't get a chance to say anything. For there was a faint shouting and banging and sound of running feet, something was happening in Timnah itself, and I jumped up on to a high rock to get a better look.

And it was a fire. Another fire. But this fire was right inside the fortified walls of Timnah. Ah, I said to myself, one of those jackals has broken in through a crack in the city walls and has started another fire.

But no, it wasn't a jackal, it was men. Men had started that fire, men were there, shouting and cursing and yelling as only men do, while the flames began to leap and lunge right into the clouds.

And Samson saw it. Samson saw it and saw what it was. For he was off down the hillside like a flash of lightning, leaping wildly from rock to rock like a great antlerless stag, the exhaustion and fatigue of these last several days now swept away in a passion that was utterly consuming.

By the time I came clambering and puffing into the town it was nearly over. The fire was in the house of Samson's wife. Just a heap of red-hot ashes. And the girl and her father were there in the ashes!

For, as with starting eyes the people saw their crops disappear in leaping flames, the answer was as simple as the question. "Who on earth did this?" "Who's to blame for this?" "Samson. He did it." "Samson, the son-in-law of the Timnite, because he gave Samson's wife to his best man."

And Samson had guessed all this. As he sat up on that rock beside me on the hilltop, as he saw the flames burst out in that house in the town, he knew. He knew it was no jackal that started that fire, he knew the Philistines well enough to be able to guess it all.

And now Samson was there, too, when I arrived, but it was nearly over. The fire was indeed right out, but the fighting was only nearly over.

What a shambles. Nothing that the Hollywood screen has ever rolled out in Technicolor or Panavision or Cinemascope or Todd-AO or all the rest of it could nearly match this. For this was real. That was not ketchup, mere tomato sauce, that was spattered all round the burnt-out house—no, that was blood. Lots of blood, Philistine blood. Those human forms in such grotesque attitudes were not models kept in the prop room for dumping about at the producer's direction—those were dead Philistines, just where they had crashed to their death under the fists and strength of Samson.

The Old Testament writer, reporting this event, just

records it in one line: "He smote them hip and thigh with great slaughter." That "great slaughter" bit is right enough, and you can say that again. But that "hip and thigh" is the understatement of all time. Sure, there was some dislocated hips and some mangled thighs, but that was merely incidental. The faces that were simply pulverised, the heads that had been slammed against the ground in a wild flailing circle of impact, the arms that had been snapped like celery sticks and hung utterly shapeless, the one poor wretch who had had a whole forearm avulsion in dehumanising disfigurement—just "hip and thigh", that's not the way I'd say it!

And Samson was alone, now. A few stones still flying at him, it is true, thrown from behind walls and doors, but he didn't even seem to notice them. It was in fact over.

Then there were feet, the feet of men running. Running away, running out of the town, out along the surrounding roadways leading to other towns. Ha! I thought, they're sending for reinforcements. They've conceded local defeat— they're calling G.H.Q. Samson, I was going to call out, this is dangerous. You'd better scram. Beat it for safety. I don't know where you ought to go, but whatever you do, get out of here. They'll bring in their archers and their artillery and goodness knows what, and you won't have a chance. Quick, run.

But Samson had already got the message, Samson was already running. Exhausted, absolutely out on his feet, Samson was still running, escaping out into the never-never, out to the cleft of the Rock of Etam ...

This time it was Samson who was in trouble. And it was certainly Trouble, capital T. For the whole sorry tale of malice and murder and mayhem reached Philistine Headquarters. And the Philistines were fighting people, one of the greatest and toughest fighting people the world has ever seen, and this burning of crops and beating-up of a whole township did not suit the Philistine system at all. Quite OK if they did it themselves, of course, but a very different matter when somebody dished it back to them.

Up from the coast, up from the main Philistine administrative area, lumbered the arresting body. Probably about a single battalion, but remember that a battalion is nothing like a mere couple of cops knocking on the door, with truncheons in their hands. Philistine troops were very heavily armed, their whole philosophy of battle depended on a concentration of headlong, helmeted, breast-plated, shielded, armoured might. And I smirked and chuckled and guffawed and finally burst out in open mocking laughter as I saw it happen. The whole battalion of them, major, captains, lieutenants, N.C.O.s and privates, were actually scared to death of him. Terrified! Those great men from the sea, those people who had Egypt bowing to them in humble recognition of their prowess, why, these fellows were thrown into a panic by one single unarmed refugee hiding in a cleft in the rock at Etam. No wonder I am laughing uproariously. For when the Spirit of God really chooses to drive a man, then you may well expect that He will also be driving a lot of ignorant Philistines, however sophisticated and up-to-date and clever and cultured—and even scientific—they might think themselves to be.

Your guess is as good as mine, of course. We're all only guessing, but this is my guess, for what it is worth. I guess that the whole story of Samson had by now been blown up into a nerve-tingling rumour that was whispering through chattering teeth from one end of Philistia to the other. "Gee, you should have seen those fellows down at Askelon. They say there were thirty of them, but I have a mate in the M.P.s there and he says there were probably hundreds. The authorities only listed thirty, but that was to save the morale of the city." "He's like a will-o'-the-wisp. Flashes all over the country like a streak of lightning. I don't believe in ghosts, of course, but by gum, he's terribly like one!" "I'm not scared of men, I tell you, I was down at the Nile invasion, and even the enormous black fellows the Gyppos had enlisted were dead enough once you ran a spear through them. But this chap's different, I tell you, and I don't mind admitting ·I'm scared."

Yes, Dame Rumour may be a lying Jade, but rumour built on fear can be the undoing of many a strong man. And the Philistine battalion was very careful to keep out of Samson's way. They headed straight for Lehi, a town in Judah.

The Judahites came out to meet them as they snapped to a sharp staccato, military halt. The mayor of Lehi himself was the spokesman. His° deference to the C.O. was genuine and unaffected. "Please, sir, tell us what is the trouble. Why are you here with all these troops?"

The Philistine major came straight to the point. "We want Samson. We want to take him and give him a taste of his own medicine. And we want you to get him for us, see? You know where he's hiding, no kidding you don't, and you just go and get him. Fast!"

The Philistines were scared, and no kidding they weren't.

But now the tribesmen of Judah had the task of taking Samson. And they didn't like the idea, either. They didn't have any military battalions, their Philistine overlords saw to that, but they managed to collect up a small army of men, several thousand strong, to go and·get Samson.

I may be wrong, but I don't think I am. I think Samson had been feeling pretty flat, all that time out there in a cleft in the rock of Etam. Thinking, wondering, remembering, reflecting.

Praying? I don't know, I would dearly love to think so; but I'm afraid it would not be true. I see a lot of people and talk to a lot of people in trouble—all my working life I do that, but not many of them are praying. I sometimes even ask them that. But not often are they praying.

No, I can't say Samson was praying. For I know that a man doesn't really start praying until in his heart he has started crying. Until great tears of true repentance are rolling down his spiritual cheeks, until great sobbing gasps of "God, be merciful to me, a sinner" are choking up his very heart. No, my guess is that Samson had not been praying. Now that is only my guess. It is God who knows, and He

hasn't told us. Whether Samson was praying or not, out
there in the cleft of the rock at Etam, we may not know,
but we do know that God was driving him hard. The Spirit
of God doesn't cease to drive in the life of a man of faith
just because the fellow doesn't bother to pray. The love and
the concern and the all-driving presence of God doesn't
depend on mere human prayer. But I think that perhaps
Samson had not really been praying.

At any rate, it was certainly a very subdued Samson who
came out of the cave in the rock to meet the motley crowd
of men from Judah.

"Good-day. What do you want?"

"Hey, listen, Samson! You've got us all in a great big
stinking mess, you have, and no denying it."

"Yes? And what makes you think that? What have I
done?"

"Aw, heck, man you're crazy. Those Philistines are our
bosses, they've got their hooks in us, right deep they have,
and you've gone and stirred up an absolute hornets' nest.
Boy, are we in trouble!"

"Yes, Samson, he's right. There is a great big army of
them in the middle of our town right now, drinking all our
beer and ready to make all the trouble in the world. And
just because of you."

Samson was feeling miserable. "Depressed" is our word.
Right down in the dumps. Like Elijah under his juniper
tree, like Jonah under his gourd, like Bunyan under the
thumb of Giant Despair. Glum. Surly.

"Aw, stow it! I was only doing to them exactly what they
did to me. Why should they moan? Lousy Philistines." And
he spat his contempt and disgust.

But the men of Judah were not to be put off. Samson in
this sombre mood was far less danger than that fully armed
detachment of Philistine troops up there in the middle of
the town square at Lehi at this moment.

"Listen, Samson, we don't like it, sure we don't. And we
don't mean you any harm, honest we don't, but we've just
got to do it. We're going to tie you up and hand you over

to them. We're sorry, we really are, but we just can't help it."

I'm guessing again, but I think that the idea of getting right in the middle of Philistine men, getting close enough to be able to feel the crack of bone under flesh, the exultation of just one more chance of pulling a Philistine limb from limb (yes, the chance of "smiting them hip and thigh", if you prefer that wrestling idiom) was something he could not resist. I am sure there was a flash in his eye and a pace in his pulse that had not been there thirty seconds before.

"No nonsense from you men? You promise you won't do anything to me yourselves? I won't have to contend with any of you at all? You swear it?"

"Sure, Samson, we mean it. We will simply tie you up and hand you over to them. We don't want to hurt you and we promise we won't hurt you."

These little "cities" in the Old Testament were really just fortresses. Some of them were so tiny that we would be better to think of them as mere pill-boxes. The people were entirely rural, no factories, offices, warehouses, no sprawling suburbs and corner gas stations and parking lots. The town square really doubled for Main Street, and that was it. Working all day in the fields, the people simply came into their tiny city to sleep in safety.

And Lehi was one of these. Perhaps as big as the Sydney cricket ground, fit nicely into the Oval, think of the stadium at Madison Square Garden—that's about how big it was. And when you crowd a whole Philistine battalion into a little spot like that, there's not a lot of free space just to kick a football. So that hours of sitting around and twiddling their thumbs and drinking the warm Lehi beer was just thoroughly boring for the Philistines. And shade was hard to find and it was altogether a hateful way to fill in a day.

And suddenly there he was. Samson! The legendary champion they had come to capture was quietly walking up towards the city gates, arms securely tied by stout new ropes. The men of Judah just fell back from following him and there he was alone. Samson, unarmed, unsupported, arms trussed to his sides, the most helpless-looking captive in all their army days.

There was a rush to reach him. Who is going to get in the first punch, who is going to be the first to blacken one of his eyes? C'mon, grab him!

And as the first Philistine soldiers poured out through the city gates, swords, spears, breast-plates, helmets and what-have-you lying in heaps in the corners of the city square, as again Samson saw Philistine faces right up close to him, as he heard the taunting sneers of Philistine voices, something in him seemed to explode. "The ropes on his arms became like burnt tow, and his bonds melted away," says the Hebrew historian, in a sudden burst of imaginative description. "The Spirit of the Lord suddenly seized him," he says in another idiom again.

And how right both imagination and idiom turn out to be. For there is a sudden heave of shoulders, a tensing of arms against trunk, and Samson is free!

The good stout new ropes just fall to the ground in shreds, and Samson springs. A crunching crack of skull on skull as the first two Philistine heads are slammed together—and then it is really on. The men at the back can't see what is happening out there in front, and they are shoving and pressing to get a better look. And as an occasional Philistine comes clearly into their view, the poor wretch just tossed into the air or just whirled around like a human club, they shove and push even harder still to get a look before it's all over.

Whew! I said before that Hollywood and its big screens has never filmed anything like that fraças at Timnah. Then Timnah was merely the scale model, Timnah was only the 8-mm home movie version. Bodies beginning to heap up around him now, Samson's hands are in danger from the very beating he is raining on jaws and noses and ribs alike. Of course in Soho and the Bronx all the experienced thugs carry knuckle-dusters and bicycle chains, but Samson is unarmed.

He is in trouble now. Never mind, Samson, I want to call out. Just keep going. Stick to it! But of course I would never be heard above that thunderous turmoil. Keep it up, I want to say, God will get you a weapon, the Spirit of the Lord is mightily upon you, Samson, and He won't leave you in the lurch. You don't know this, of course, but you are in fact part of the softening-up process God is going to use to end the whole history of Philistia—your mother knows that, she was told it at the time of your birth. But neither your mum nor your dad would ever have imagined it would work out like this.

But I can't talk to Samson, and he couldn't hear me if I were able, and in any case he's got too much to think about, for his fists and his hands won't take much more punishment. Oh, God, I'm saying, can't You do something? Quick, God, get cracking with some scheme to help him. Bring back a few hundred of those cowardly Judahites, anything, Samson's knuckles won't stand it much more. Oh, please, God, can't you …

And he sees it! There, on the ground, right beside his dancing feet as he leaps and lunges and jumps and side-steps, there, right there, is a great big bone. A jawbone. A nice fresh, not too brittle jawbone. The donkey who used to own it has gone, but here is his last and perfect gift to Samson. He has his knuckle-duster.

And now it is just one-sided the other way. Samson is now actually chasing them, having to advance towards the still packed gateway to find men to kill. A huge stack of maimed, bloody corpses on his right and on his left, where he has tossed them as he cracked ribs and skulls, an even larger pile behind him where he literally hooked them over his shoulders in murderous two-handed wallops to belly and chin. And only the forward-pressing Philistines in the actual gateway to face.

It is only a matter of time, of course. It can't go on inde-finitely. Samson could go on indefinitely, he isn't cracking up or slowing down or calling it a day. No. It isn't Samson, it is the Philistines who are beginning to lose their taste for it. The cries and the grunts and the shrieks are all Philistine, even the fellows right at the back of the crowd are beginning to realise this, and slowly the truth begins to sink in. They are being massacred! Their whole battalion is being wiped out. And by a single man!

And it is over. A sudden turn of face and the men in the gateway spring back to safety and slam the city doors. They are licked.

And Samson is free. He looks at the jawbone still held in murderous strength in his right hand and gives a great exultant laugh.

"With the jawbone of an ass, I have flayed them like asses."

Then he looks around again at the piles of men lying in such ghastly death, and there is something that is sheer wonderment, true awe, as he barely whispers,

"With the jawbone of an ass I have slain a thousand men."

I think he will break down, he looks so tired and tense, and yet so flushed and excited. But a sudden quick flick of his hand and the blood-soaked jawbone goes hurtling high over the city walls among the few terrified Philistines inside. He just turns and walks away, right to the top of a small nearby hill, where he sits down wearily at last.

I begin to walk slowly up the hillside, wondering just how Samson must be feeling. He must be tremendously exhilarated, of course; he could not possibly be unalert to the sheer fantasy of this afternoon's performance. But does he know how mightily the spirit of the Lord seized him? I wonder if he's on his knees, thanking God for all that happened.

And I quicken my pace as I get near, and then I start to run, to come sprinting up as fast as my old legs will carry me.

For Samson is in fact on his knees. He is indeed talking to God. "Hurrah!" I exclaim, "Samson must be praying to God at last! Let me hear!"

Yes. Samson is on his knees, he is talking to God. But not praying, he's complaining. Complaining to God! "God," he's saying, "what a fat lot of good this has all turned out to be. You have given me a most spectacular victory and deliverance, and just what on earth is the use? For here I am, dead-beat and dying of thirst. All the heathenish Philistines have to do is walk up and take me. I simply can't go another step. I'm just dying of thirst."

And something in me nearly snaps. I feel that I've heard more than a human can stand. The weariness, the exhaustion, the state of utter collapse—this I can understand, can recognise in deepest sympathy. But this ingratitude, this final indirected selfishness, is the limit. God will just let him die, I'm muttering to myself, and so He should. God must be absolutely fed up with him, big muscles and passions and hormones and all that he has, I'll bet God will just wipe him out.

And I hear a noise—I think it's a pebble falling. Then a clatter as some rocks topple over, boulder upon boulder. This is it, I say, it's an earthquake or a land slide or something, God is going to finish him, and serve him jolly well right. And I look round, and Samson looks too, to see what it is—and it's water. Cool, clear, spring water now bubbling merrily out of a crevice in the rock face. And Samson is there, his face bowed down to the cooling, life-saving water. And I bow, too, altogether overwhelmed by the endless patience and kindness and gentleness of God. The God who can speak to the Philistines in the flashing jawbone of an ass, is the same God who speaks so sweetly and refreshingly to Samson in En-hakkore, "the Crier's Spring".

Samson is in no-man's-land. Manoah, his old father, and his excitable old mother—these old people are now far distant from him. Their narrowness, their slavish adherence to their vows and their rituals and their tedious restrictions —yes, he doesn't belong there now.

And the Philistines, the big sea people with their wealth and their culture and their sophistication—no, he just can't belong to them, however much he tries.

No-man's-land. He doesn't like the old life at home—he

just can't stomach the Philistine life when he meets it: it's got to be no-man's-land.

I don't know how long Samson lived like this. Probably the best part of twenty years, in all, twenty years of searching and wandering and homelessness. Of how he fared, all this long time in this spiritual no-man's-land, we hardly know a single thing. Or, more exactly, we know only one single thing.

That one single thing happened at Gaza. I don't know when he went to Gaza. I can't for the life of me imagine why he went to Gaza, but there he was. Gaza was the very furthest Philistine capital from his home country. It seems he had got as far, as very far, as he could get. But when or why, there he was at Gaza.

And what was he actually doing, now that he was there? Simple question, obvious answer—a woman.

Poor Samson. All those enormous passions and moods and driving urges, fancy coming away down here to Gaza to try and find the deep satisfying fulfilment that would never come to him again. For the girl was a prostitute. She was just for sale. But she was a woman, and he would have to be content at that. No fine townsfolk willing to accept this long-haired, bearded giant of a man into their Philistine home, of course. Not after Timnah; certainly not after Askelon; you could bet your life on it, not after Lehi. Only a matter of time and the secret of who he was must out, the Philistine military junta would latch on to him, and that would be that. No, no respectable, reputable Philistine beauty for a sweetheart. Just a prostitute.

And even then the news leaked out. The civic bosses got the tip-off, they found out: Samson is here. Samson in there with that black-eyed girl in the third house on the left. Samson!

What a dramatic turn. What a fantastic bit of luck—Samson's here, what say we go and kill him? Yes, men, what say we go and kill him? OK, mate, in you go. But don't forget what happened in Lehi—hadn't you better go and frisk him for jawbones? And at Askelon—just killed them in the streets. And at Timnah there was hardly a single skull without a crack in it! Sure, let's go and kill him. But you go first!

Hmmm. Not so easy, is it? But he's there, and we don't want to miss him. Well ... we'd better wait till daylight. Yes, that's a good sound idea. Wait till we can see, and then do it all safely. OK, that's what we'll do. But go and lock the town gates. Put a good iron chain on them and wait till morning.

And there is Samson, up in the room with the prostitute, the gates of the city bolted and locked and the whole of Gaza under armed guard ...

But sex without love is poor company, lust is sadly and utterly lonely. So that it was only midnight and Samson was going. No one, now, to keep him in Gaza, even though it was only midnight. And Samson came to the city gates all bound and bolted, to find himself a prisoner. A captive, now, inside the main city of all ancient Philistia.

Samson, a captive. Caught at last, trapped inside Gaza itself.

And in the shock and the challenge and the threat he threw himself straight at the doors themselves. And in one mighty convulsive heave he had the doors and the door-posts, barred and chained, lintel and all, clean out of the ground and hoisted on to his shoulders. And away with them he raced, up hill, down dale, clean across country to the top of the hill outside Hebron—thirty-eight miles. Thirty-eight miles he lumped those doors, and then tossed them on the hilltop!

Sure, we know only one single thing that happened in all that long, sad, twenty years in no-man's-land—but that one thing was quite a something.

Samson didn't have a clue in the world as to how or where or why his strength belonged to him. He thought he knew, sure he did, but he was miles out, really. He thought it was his hair. Shades of all the physiologists and endocrinologists in the history of medical science. But Samson was really convinced that his strength lay in his whiskers. Now when you have stopped chuckling over that crazy idea, I must insist that it's not in any sense as wicked or dangerous as could be, even though it is certainly as wrong as could be. Remember, it's not many years at all since lots of intelligent people were quite sure you could measure a man's brains and character by the bumps on his head. No, Samson may have been wrong, but he was not wicked.

For of course the actual source of his strength lay in the fact of his relationship to God. His strength came from the unique equipment that God had designed into him and now operated within him in His indwelling power. He was a true Nazirite.

But Samson thought, as his mother and father seemed to think, that he could become a Nazirite by virtue of just keeping some rules about grog and haircuts and shaving and dead bodies. Just a sort of trick that could be played with certain symbols. Like algebra, if you think back to some schoolday memories:

Find the roots of the quadratic expression $ax^2 + bx + c = 0$

If $\quad ax^2 + bx + c = 0$

$\therefore 4a^2x^2 + 4abx + 4ac = 0$ (multiplying by $4a$)

$\therefore 4a^2x^2 + 4abx + b^2 = b^2 - 4ac$

i.e. $\quad (2ax + b)^2 = b^2 - 4ac$

$\therefore ax + b = \pm (b^2 - 4ac)^{\frac{1}{2}}$ by taking the root.

$\therefore 2ax = -b \pm (b^2 - 4ac)^{\frac{1}{2}}$

$$\therefore x = \frac{-b \pm (b^2 - 4ac)^{\frac{1}{2}}}{2a}$$

I'm sure that's what Manoah and his wife really thought. Keep the rules, don't drink, etc., and you're a Nazirite, as if God were a mathematician who passed and failed his subjects by a process of spiritual mathematics.

And Samson had been brought up with that idea. Samson, don't cut your hair; Samson, don't eat that salad, it's got cucumber in it; Samson, don't drink that punch, it's got wine in it; no, Samson, dear, granny's dead, and we are Nazirite people, we don't go and look at dead bodies, only people who aren't Nazirites do that sort of thing.

Just a set of rules. Just religious algebra. And when he walked through the vineyard at Timnah, when he killed the lion, when he actually ate the honey out of the dead lion (and so did mum and dad) and then after all that when he found that he could still stave in a Philistine sternum and still crack a Philistine mandible—why, he argued, the strength must lie in his hair, that was the only little bit of algebra—I mean Nazirite vow—remaining.

Samson was wrong, but he was only one of a vast number of people of all ages who make the same mistake.

For of course the truth is that his strength lay in God. God made him strong. Now I'm not questioning that God's way of making him strong was by providing him with some absolutely fantastic physiological machinery. Fantastic is the word. Unique. But I'm equally certain that this fantastic physiological machinery wouldn't have petered out just by shaving, any more than it didn't peter out when he strolled through a vineyard or ate honey out of a dead lion's carcass. Of course not.

But Samson didn't know all this, he didn't really know that the Spirit of God was driving him, that the Spirit of the Lord could actually fill a man with those limitless capacities as God needed him to have them. And, what is almost more important still, Samson didn't know that God the Holy Spirit could wipe that whole strength out at a moment's notice.

No, Samson did not know that, but it was getting near the time for God to show him that. For in the endless wonder of the love of God, no man will ever be allowed to believe that his strength is in fact in himself, that he can in any way be his own saviour.

And the story of Samson is coming to an end. When any man finally discovers the great truth that all his strength must lie in God, when his whole being is finally handed over to the will of God, then that man's story is truly at an end. That man is as good as dead. In spiritual fact, that man is dead. For then, and then only, does that man really live. "The man who loves himself is lost, but he who hates himself in this world will be kept safe for eternal life" was how Jesus said this, of you, of me, of Samson, and of Himself. This is the law of life in God.

And now Samson is going to find this law at work in himself.

Yes, it's getting near the end. The drive of the Spirit of God has never let up, God never does let up, of course, but the last hard bit of driving is almost complete. Not that Samson is old—he's barely middle-aged. But God is concerned with a man's life, not his age, and God's driving was to take its last tremendous turn.

And to do that, the Spirit of God took him to Sorek.

Samson is down in Sorek. This is not home, but it's quite near to home. And what machinery did God use to take him to Sorek? Need you ask. What takes Samson anywhere? In fact, to be brutally honest, what takes almost any man anywhere?

Of course! And Samson's woman was Delilah. Samson loved Delilah. She was probably an Israelite. Her name is Semitic, the pundits assure us, and there she was in Sorek with Samson. And perhaps we feel we can relax, we can unwind a bit and think how lucky it is, after all that early trouble, why, here Samson is, all settled down at last, comfortable little home, and his Delilah, the girl he loves, there to keep house for him and bring him some children and simple undisturbed contentment. Yes, there's Samson in Sorek.

Samson and Delilah. Perhaps the generous-hearted Israelites will make a warm place for him, perhaps even the big-time Philistines will just forget about a solitary misfit like him and leave him alone at last.

Yes, all very nice and comfortable and cosy indeed. Except for one single thing: except for the fact that it was not true.

For there were no Israelite neighbours popping in to say hello and is there anything I can do to help you settle down, we're just two doors down from you and want to make you feel welcome and we'll see you at the evening sacrifice? No. Not Samson. Not Samson and Delilah in Sorek. No

Israelite visitors.

But plenty of Philistine visitors. They had not forgotten Samson, not for one tiny moment. Their spies were everywhere, and Samson was right up at the top of their "Men Wanted" list. Philistines were literally crawling all over the place just about any old time they liked. The whole place was just dripping with Philistines.

But they didn't come to see Samson. Philistines who came to see Samson need only buy a one-way ticket, no use just wasting cash on buying a return for home. Samson still couldn't resist a Philistine skull or rib-cage. No, they came to see Delilah. She was the one. Samson loved Delilah, but Delilah loved money, and the Philistines had the dough.

Until it was the Philistine lords themselves who came to make the big deal. Five Philistine warlords, there were, and it seems that she had a visit from all five of them. Just imagine, little Mrs. Housewife hanging out the washing one Monday morning and up rolled the whole war cabinet.

And they made their proposition ...

When a really superior, high-class, upper-crust, socially grade-A girl married in that culture, she brought a proper dowry with her. It was hers, and she brought it into her new home. No Savings Bank account, no script for gilt-edged shares, of course. And no minted cash, either, for there were no real coins or anything like that.

But it was silver. Pieces of silver, good negotiable assets always, and the best tradition called for eleven bundles of silver pieces. Each bundle may in fact consist of a hundred such pieces, but there would be eleven such small bundles. And the best girls had that as a dowry. If you kept up with the Philistine-Joneses next door, your daughter had eleven hundred pieces of silver.

And the warlords came to Delilah and offered her eleven hundred pieces of silver. Each! Five rich, rare, valuable silver dowries! And she was a Hebrew by name and background, she was a member of a tiny subject race, and offered five—one, two, three, four, *five*—dowries.

And the payment was to be made for Samson. Find out
from him the secret of his strength, find out from him
how to tame him and then get him tamed—and the cash
was hers. That was their bargain, the cheating Philistine
nobles.

And Delilah accepted. She was a Philistine at heart, for
sure she was, Hebrew name and all, and she made a deal of
it. Sell the man who loved her for ready cash, for pride, for
anything at all, just so long as you get well paid. OK, she'll
sell Samson!

And while I take a deep breath, let me get it on the record
that those Philistines haven't changed one iota, not even
up to this late twentieth century.

I need a deep breath. I need a lot more than that, really, for
I don't want to go over that story. In some measure that
story is splashed over every page in every newspaper, it's
the stock-in-trade of every social worker, constable, lawyer
—and doctor. The sad story of the unity that is a man–
woman being divided into two by the greed or the lust
or the pride or the simple selfishness of man, of woman.

Yet there is something rather whimsical, almost funny,
even, in that story. Whimsical, funny, that is, if you can read
it as a piece of entertainment, as a bit of an outline for a
T.V. sketch or a celluloid drama. That pretence of Samson's
about tying him up with seven brand new unstretched bowstrings and he would be as weak as a kitten. Pouff! He
snapped those bowstrings before he even realised that his
sneaky little two-timing lady love had got them on him!
And then that bit about the new ropes—it's really quite a
laugh—why, he had come up to Lehi bound by two new
ropes, and that's where he beat up that whole Philistine
battalion. Very funny.

And the day she wove all his hair, yard by yard by endless yard, into a great whiskery mat all laced within the
intricacy of the entire weaving loom. Surely one of the
zaniest sights this world has ever seen, as Samson leaped to
his feet with that whole quarter of a ton of loom-makers'

bric-à-brac dangling from his scalp. Boy, oh boy, but that was a scream! It had the fans rolling in the aisles, it got the box-office absolutely spinning with doubloons as they stacked the public in.

Sure, very funny. Very funny indeed, if it were at the Tivoli, if it were Hollywood, if it were Stratford-on-Avon.

But it's really the end. It's not a comedy, it's not even entertainment at all—it's the final driving revolution of the Sprit of God as He brings the story of Samson to its close. And I can hardly trust myself to look, as Delilah goes to meet the Philistine lords for the last time. "No slip-up this time," she says, "this is the real thing. I've pumped the absolute heart out of the clot, I've got the secret this time. You come up to my place tonight, and bring the cash with you, five complete dowries, remember, and no monkey tricks about the payment."

For Samson had broken right down. The last little bit of Nazirite bond, the final tie that he had tried to keep between himself and God, was now broken—he had forever renounced all allegiance to his old traditions and the things that came from his mother and father. It is now Samson *vis-à-vis* God, and Samson *vis-à-vis* God alone. It had taken the wiles and the cunning and the enchantment of a Delilah to bring Samson to the place where now he must meet God on his own.

And in a treachery of love-making that was sheer ruthless murder, Samson was taken. Asleep in the gentle embrace of her woman's lap, caressed by the tenderness of her two soft breasts, lured by all the charm that only a loved one can exert on her lover, Delilah betrayed Samson.

No wonder the imagination of poets and painters and dramatists and composers in all ages has been captured by this cruel, tragic scene. Samson, asleep, his great mane of hair in the embrace of her lap, and Delilah is beckoning to the hiding Philistines to creep in and shave off all his hair. Seven great locks, that was the arrangement of his hair-do, and one by one they slipped to the floor. Until at last his head was bare, his last Nazirite symbol was taken from him. Samson was indeed alone with God.

And God left him. In the utter loneliness that alone allows true repentance, in the ashen bitterness that at last belongs to every man who has come to himself, Samson's enormous strength was gone.

"Oh, come on, doctor," you are perhaps saying, "tell us what you think happened. Could it have been a curare-like relaxant drug that had somehow got mixed up in the evening meal? Even a psychedelic? Something like marijuana? Opium? Something that reduced Samson to a mere man-sized strength? What do you think?"

I'm sorry. I can guess and you can guess, but guessing it must only ever be. But God wasn't guessing. God was driving him very hard, now, the Spirit of God was moving in this so-strange way, as Samson was brought where I must be brought and where you must be brought—because it is where Christ Himself was brought—if ever we are to receive the full glory that belongs to a son of God. It is only the man who loses his life who may hope to find life. It is only the grain of wheat that dies that may rise to the splendour of the rich, full ear. If indeed it be true that the simple biological law of life on earth is seen in the inevitability of death, then how vastly greater is the truth that the spiritual law of death in Christ is the certainty of life.

Never mind, then, the question of the mere mechanism of his physical strength, let us watch with bated breath and bowed head as we see the wonder of the greater concern of God for his new and spirit life.

For God is leaving Samson now, the Spirit of God is removing all the strength that had been filling him for nearly forty years.

And Delilah, the most wretched little Mata Hari of all history, nestles his head in her lap as she cuddles him to his doom. And then in the evil mockery and brittle scorn of her greed she wakes him in a burst of taunting torment. "Samson," she mocks, shaking him and slapping him and sneering her derision, "Samson, the Philistines are upon you. Samson!"

"He woke from his sleep and said, 'I will go out as usual and shake myself'; he did not know that the Lord had left him. The Philistines seized him, gouged out his eyes ..."

I can only suppose that Delilah got her price. I just like to think that the Philistine lords did not cheat her of the miserable pieces of silver that were her bargain for Samson's life. I can hardly bear to think of that sad, treacherous greed missing out on the baubles and trinkets that the Delilahs of life value so greatly. Yes, I just suppose Delilah got the cash.

But I know what Samson got, I'm not merely supposing that—he got blindness. The searing agony of both eyes "gouged out". The sharp, piercing eyes that could catch a young lion in its leap, that could hunt down and trap all those hundreds of jackals—just "gouged out".

And in the weakness that now fills him, as the God Who is his strength just leaves him, the great Samson is blind, and now Samson is in fetters. Enormous bronze shackles are snapped round ankles and wrists and Samson is a captive ...

It was to Gaza that he was taken. To proud, ancient Gaza, the city he had once so humiliated as he strode off with her gates and gate-posts and bars and lintel and all—it is now in Gaza that we find Samson. Grinding at the mill in the prison, in the mockery of slavery, fettered, blind.

And something tugs at my very heart as I see this, something inside me wants to break in pieces, as I feel the tragedy and the pathos and the sheer bitterness of his terrible lot. Oh, God! Oh, Christ! Oh, my Master, I want to say, I know this is the way You Yourself walked, I know Your way is the best way because it is the only way. But I'm only human, and poor Samson is only human, remarkable though he is—can't you make it a bit easier?

And I bow my head and hold my hand over my mouth, for I remember that He was human too, those were human feet that staggered up Golgotha, those were human hands that were pinned to the rough jagged plank by those merciless iron spikes, that was human flesh that had been flogged to blood-raw agony by the skin-tearing fury of the Roman scourge.

Until I am too sick at heart even to wonder any longer. A leaden heaviness fills my whole thought and mind, as I see Samson treading round and round and round in the deadly monotony of the treadmill. This fantastic physique that once let him run for hour after effortless hour, that could leap into incredible feats of prowess and valour, now held by great bronze manacles to the endless march of the mill.

And I am too numbed to think. It's all too sad and too cruel to make me even want to think. I'd just like to find time and quiet in which to lament. But I can't. For there is a bustle and an activity and a commotion in the city. Gaza is in festival array, the whole place is now buzzing with excitement and good cheer.

It is the occasion of a great Philistine festival, the festival to Dagon. The whole place is in a state of wild exultation, as their nobles call for a great time of thanksgiving for the capture of Samson. The whole nation is rejoicing.

And there, in the great City Hall in the centre of Gaza itself, the festivities come to a climax. For there will be the gathering of all the greatest in the nation, the lords and their ladies, the military top brass, the rich merchants and the district overseers, all the v.i.p.s of mighty Philistia are assembling to celebrate.

Until the hall is filled, every seat taken, every gallery packed. And as the entertainment and the carousing and the excitement mounts, a call is heard. "Samson!" "Bring in Samson!" "Samson!" "We want Samson." And now feet are tapping it and hands are clapping it as great Philistine voices are shouting it. "We want Samson! We want Samson! We want Samson!"

And in a sudden frenzy of clamour and applause, Samson appears. There, down in the very centre of this great oval hall, with its high tiered galleries supported by the two mighty timber pillars, there is Samson. Blind, bound, fettered, but it is Samson none the less. Those broad shoulders, those rippling muscles that flex and curve with the grace and speed that once so terrified every man and woman in the land, these can only ever belong to Samson. And that great head with its enormous shock of hair—why, that's Samson, even if the flashing glint of eye is gone in the ghastly hollowness of the sockets from which the eyes have been gouged. Yes, his eyes are gone, gone for ever; but his hair has grown, the beard is there again, it is Samson. "Hurrah! It's Samson!" "Yes, Samson! Make him play some tricks! Make sport of him! Dish it out to him, this time! It's his turn now!"

And now I can't see much at all myself. Not because of the throng, not because of those enormous central pillars, but because I'm so nearly blind myself. Because of the unashamed blinking that alone can allow me sight at all.

Until the whole place is thundering as if to breaking-point. I look up hurriedly to see if the rafters can take the strain, as thousands of richly booted feet are stamping a deafening accompaniment to the uproarious shouting and screaming of that vast assembly of great ones. But the building does not do more than tremble with the violence of the tumult, walls and pillars stand intact, as Samson is led on to the central plinth on which the very pillars themselves stand. And the lad who leads him in is cocking up an ear to try and hear him, Samson is saying something to him through the din and the turmoil. Why, yes, the boy is showing blind Samson where the two great pillars are, the mighty Samson is leaning on the pillars as if for support. Surely Samson is not worn out with weariness, surely his proud head is not bowed with despair.

Samson, I call out, trying to make myself heard above all these thousands of Philistine voices, Samson, don't despair. Don't give up in despondency and depression. God has left you, Samson, but not to destroy you. He is only ever wanting to save you. But while ever you think you have strength to save yourself, He is powerless to help. Samson, abandon your own freedom, slave that you are, and seek the bondage of God that alone makes real liberty.

So I turn at last to face him. And I stare, dry-eyed, now, in an open-eyed gaze that is as unashamed as the blinking of a minute ago. For Samson is praying. Yes, Samson is praying. At last, at long, sad, but exciting last, Samson is really turning to God. All that life-long driving and caring of the Spirit of God is being fulfilled, Samson is in the will of God. This is Saint Paul in the sixth of Romans! This is the parable of the Prodigal in Luke fifteen! This is the wonder of all creation, that man who is animal may find a place in the very heart of God who is Spirit. This, in simple fact, is the Gospel.

"O Lord God, remember me," Samson is praying. Samson now belongs to God. And all the courage and all the adventure and even the laughing gaiety is still there, for God never destroys those who trust in Him, He only ever perfects them. Yes, all those qualities of greatness that were there in Samson the man are still there as in repentance and faith he becomes Samson the Son of God. Samson, the Son of God. He's praying again. Not heard by human ears, deafened as they are by all the noise, but heard so clearly by God. Listen: "Remember me, O Lord God, remember me: give me the strength only this once, O God, and let me at one stroke be avenged on the Philistines for my two eyes."

And with the great surging burst of strength that fills a man when he knows the dynamic of being at peace with God, Samson grasps the two pillars and skids them from their footing on the stone plinth where he stands between them.

And in this structural instability of architectural design that has ever since amazed both archaeologists and engineers alike, down crashed the enormous edifice. Out of the vast galleries high above his head spilled the whole of the gentry of Philistia, crashing to their doom on the sea of terror-stricken people below.

And so died Samson, no longer a mere Nazirite, never a Philistine, altogether a man of faith ...

Larrikin? Scalliwag? Just a great big bullying over-muscled lout? Is that what you think? "His life seems to have revolved around illicit relationships with prostitutes and loose-living women ... a sad tale of a lack of discipline and true devotion"—and I'm actually quoting here, you notice—is that your opinion too?

Sure, you're entitled to your opinion, and it may be as right as the opinion of anybody else. You stick to your opinion, of course, you're fully entitled to it.

But it's God's opinion I'm interested in. After all those twenty and more years of driving hard by the Spirit of God, what does God finally think of Samson? Thumbs down? Failed? Not worthy of a place in the team? Not good enough to satisfy the heavenly examiners?

And everything in me is urging me to leap to my feet and cheer exultantly—for God has put Samson in the eleventh chapter of the Epistle to the Hebrews. Samson is in that all-famous hall of fame, the ultra-select fourteen-man list of men of faith. Read, if ever you can, of Enoch: "It is the testimony of Scripture that before he was taken he had pleased God"—and Samson is bracketed with Enoch. Read of the early patriarchs: "God is not ashamed to be called their God"—and Samson is listed with them. Moses "considered the stigma that rests on God's Anointed greater wealth than the treasures of Egypt"; Moses was "as one who saw the invisible God"—and Samson stands there alongside Moses, the great Moses himself. Rahab was a prostitute —but "she escaped the doom of the unbelievers"—along with Samson.

Yes, Samson is one of God's own men! And God sums them all up with this tremendous accolade: "They were too good for this world." That is God's judgment.

And now everything that is in me is urging me to fall on my knees in sheer adoration and wonder at the limitless love of God. For God has never picked his men because they are good enough to gain his approval: He has only ever accepted men because they are needy enough to seek His forgiveness. That is what God is like! That is the truth about God who is *God*. Not checking men's dossiers to be sure they are perfect, but accepting men in their willingness to allow Him to make them perfect.

And that is what God has been showing me in the life of Samson. Choosing this turbulent, reactionary, deeply disturbed lad from the home of poor old Manoah and his excitable wife, and patiently driving and driving in the life and affairs of this so mixed-up kid, as He set out on the eternal purpose of perfecting him. That is the real story of Samson, just as it is the story of any and of every saint of God.

GOD SEES IN THE DARK

Jesus once said: "The lamp of the body is the eye. If your eyes are sound, you will have light for your whole body: if the eyes are bad, your whole body will be in darkness. If then the only light you have is darkness, the darkness is doubly dark."

Now the Book of Judges concludes with two almost unbelievable stories that will make this profound truth so clear, so frighteningly clear, that nobody may ever plead ignorance of it. Two simple, crude, ever-so-human stories, yet telling us something that God would always have men know about themselves and light ...

The first story concerns the tribe of Dan. You may remember that Samson came from the tribe of Dan, that most insignificant of all the tribes, the one that didn't even have a piece of countryside of its own. There they were, squatting in the cramped-up discomfort of sharing their affairs with whatever Judah and Benjamin pleased to concede to them. And the Danites did not—repeat not—like it. So they determined to do something about it.

But the story really begins up in the hill country of Ephraim, quite a long way to their north. In the rugged loneliness of the inhospitable hill country, there lived a man called Micah. And the happenings all centred about Micah.

Now there are several Micah's in the Bible, but three of them get a special mention. One was a prophet in Ahab's time, and the last we see of him is as he is being dragged off to prison—and we don't hear of his release. The second is Micah the Minor Prophet—he's the one everybody knows a bit about. He was a young contemporary of Isaiah, and if you went to Sunday School or listened to sermons much, or sang Wesley's hymns or attended Bible study circles—then you will almost certainly know Micah the Minor Prophet.

I was barely a teenager myself when I first met up with this
Micah: "Who is a pardoning God like Thee, and who has
grace so rich and free?" Do you know that chorus? Then
it is based on a text taken from Micah's prophecy. And I
couldn't possibly count or remember the choruses and sermons and talks I have heard on the text: "Thou wilt cast
all their sins into the depths of the sea"—also from Micah
the prophet. But the Micah of this story is the other one.

For in all my life so far (and that's most of it) I have never
heard a single reference from pulpit or song writer or study
leader or anybody else at all—never one single tiny whispered
sound—that relates to the Micah of the Book of Judges.

For this Micah was an obscure little farmer living away
out in this desolate Ephraim hill country over four hundred
years before Isaiah. A nobody. Just a speck on the whole
social calendar. But that is not why his name is not even
whispered. Not at all. The reason is that the story is so
crazy, so mixed-up that obviously the parsons and clerics are
too embarrassed by it to let out a single peep. And don't
think I am being hard on them—not a bit. Even the writer
of the Book of Judges is embarrassed by it. As we will see,
even he finds it almost impossible now and again to go on
with the account, it is so obviously hard for him to realise
in the topsy-turvy affairs of people like this, that God is in
fact God, that God is not made in our image.

Micah's mother lost her dowry.

I can't help thinking that the old lady may well have been
a Philistine, because the dowry was the very same "eleven
hundred pieces of silver" that Delilah got five times over
for Samson. Real Philistine-sized wealth. I'm only guessing
that, I admit, but any woman living in the struggling penury
of the hill country of Ephraim who could flash a complete,
genuine eleven-hundred-pieces-of-silver dowry was unusual
to say the least. But she had had her dowry. And now she
had lost it.

Imagine the commotion and the consternation she caused
as she burst into the kitchen right in the middle of the family

breakfast one morning. "Listen! I've lost my dowry! All of my dowry is gone." And a quick dab to dry her free-coursing tears and a quick wipe to mop up her sniffling nose. "And now I've put a curse on it. Somebody has stolen it. I just know some miserable wretch has stolen it, and I have cursed it!" The words just spat themselves out; but she was far too worked up to stop. "It's a terrible curse, and anybody who tries to use the dowry will be in trouble now it's an awful curse and it will serve him right the dirty rat I hope it strikes him dead." And the sudden burst of hate-filled eloquence dissolved in a flood of sobs and groans. You couldn't even hear little Joe slurping the milk in the bottom of his porridge bowl.

There was just the dramatic response that you would expect. The "Ohhh" and the "Tch tch" and the "Heavens above" and the "Goodness gracious me" that any family circle would express after an announcement like this. As the daughters and the grand-daughters hugged her and told her not to worry and it will turn up and all the rest of such comfortless comfort, the sons and grandsons looked grim and said what a lousy thing to do and what sort of a skunk much this be to do such a mean thing to a poor old innocent lady who had never even hurt a fly in all her life and what a jolly good thing it was that she had had the sense to slap on that curse and they all hoped the curse was really power-ful and they all felt a whole lot better as they began to imagine the torture and wretchedness a real Grade-A curse can land on a man.

Yes, they all felt a lot better. All except Micah.

For Micah was looking slightly green about the gills and swallowing large gulps of air and altogether sinking into a state of near-collapse. Until at last he could stand it no longer, and in a reedy voice and with trembling lips he croaked, "Mother. That dowry. That dowry with the curse on it, you've just told us about. Mother, I've got it. I ... er, that is ... I ... I took it!"

Poor Micah. No wonder the padres don't make him the hero of their sermons.

The miserable clot who stole his poor old mother's savings. What a king-sized rat this yegg must be.

And the scowls and hisses from the whole family were
entirely swept away by mother herself. For she just ran
across the room and threw her arms around his neck in the
warmest possible motherly hug and kissed him and kissed
him. "Micah, what a darling boy you are! Oh, Micah, I'm
so glad!"

Of course a middle-aged man like Micah had long ago
learned how utterly unpredictable a mother's feelings may
be. But as he went and brought the dowry even he was not
quite ready for her next move.

For as she took the precious silver, her smiles now beam-
ing through her drying tears, she burst out again: "Oh,
Micah! This is just wonderful!" And she clasped the little
bundle in both hands and dropped her gaze as she said ever
so seriously; "And I now pronounce a special blessing. I
consecrate this silver to God. And I place it in my son
Micah's hands to make two images, one overlaid in silver,
and one in solid cast silver." And she raised her old head
and looked straight at Micah as she thrust the treasure back
into his hands. "Here you are Micah. It's for you."

Well! What a breakfast scene. I just hope somebody had
the sense to make some fresh coffee. A little dose of extra
caffein all round would be very welcome.

For they were centuries before sermons from Westminster
and Rome, the name of Billy Graham would mean exactly
nothing to them—but they did know their religion. They
all knew that a curse meant that the silver couldn't just be
paid out as a down-payment on a new piece of machinery
or ordinary merchandise—the magic of a curse tied that cash
up more tightly than any covenant or document in all our
modern legal world can do today. But they also knew that
a blessing carried a higher voltage still—it could completely
over-ride the restrictions of a curse: though it also meant
that the money must now be spent on religion. It was
"blessed", it wasn't just available for general farm improve-
ments.

Sure, these were only ignorant hill-people away up in the back-blocks of the Ephraim mountains, but they were devout, serious, deeply religious people, and they did at least know that.

And Micah was now on a spending spree. Two of the eleven heaps of silver went straight to the silversmith to make up into images. The ephod was first made of wood, then the wood was overlaid in beaten silver. The teraphim was cast in solid silver. There they were, two beautiful little idols, as solemn and significant as any spire or arch or crucifix our western world would later make from the same simple superstitions.

But an ephod and a teraphim are not enough—sacred things like these can't be left on the mantelpiece for just any old visiting nobody to gaze at. Ephods and teraphim are religious, and need a religious setting. So Micah got a splendid shrine built also, and there the two silver figures were placed, all just right and correct and proper.

And then Micah had one last brilliant idea. (He had plenty of ready cash left, remember, and nothing helps the development of religious progress like adequate cash.) All this beautiful religion, two silver figures plus shrine complete—why, that all takes expert handling and care—what about getting somebody to look after it? Some one who would learn to work it and do the right things that a man should do with religion?

Of course! The answer was obvious. One of his sons—make one of his boys into a priest—just *so* obvious. And there now is Micah, one of his sons appointed to this important task, officially installed as priest, man-in-charge of all this wonderful equipment ...

And I can hear the low muttering of the old historian as he finds that he has to write this—his sheer frustration and disillusionment and dismay that such ignorance and superstition and darkness should come into the lives of the very people of God. Fancy God's chosen people not knowing better and not doing better than that. The simple human littleness and crudity of the story of Ehud; the sheer greatness of God, as seen in the stories of Barak and Gideon; the unspeakable tenderness of the love and forgiveness of God as seen in the contrasting stories of Jephthah and Samson—all this he could write without comment, it is so much to be expected, if God is really God, if only we can remember that man is merely man. Yes, that is easy, that is all wonderful, to write. But this! This disturbing darkness where there should be clear strong light—how can he make this clear? And I am sure there is a catch in his throat as he tries to explain it: "In those days there was no king in Israel and every man did what was right in his own eyes."

So Micah goes about his business, occupied in the work of his farm and in the general needs about his place. There he is, idols, shrine, son-priest installed as operator, the happiest man in all the hill country of Ephraim.

Until one day on to this scene came a visitor. The visitor was a young man from the Benjamite territory, a Levite named Jonathan. He was a priest, but priests in Benjamin were having a very tough time, very tough indeed, and young Jonathan was feeling the pinch. So here he was, tramping through the hill country of Ephraim, his swag on his back, looking for a job.

And this morning he arrived at Micah's place. "Good morning. You're a stranger in these parts? Come and have a cup of tea with us. It's hot and dusty, and you must be ready for a drink."

The young man voiced his willing acceptance and they sat down under a shady tree for the welcome tea-break.

"Where do you come from?" Micah asked with genuine interest and concern.

"My name is Jonathan, I'm a direct descendant of Gershom, and I'm not really going anywhere in particular. I'm just footloose until I can find some sort of a job. Actually I'm a Levite, and what I should be doing is trying to find a place where I can serve as a priest."

Micah's eyes widened. A priest. A genuine priest. A

proper, legitimate, real-life Levite priest! "Here," he said, rising quickly, "come and I'll show you something." And he jumped to his feet and hurried excitedly to the opposite side of his little homesite. For there, slightly hidden behind the house, out of sight of the prying of merely inquisitive eyes, in all its glory, stood the shrine enclosing the two silver images.

And now it was the young Levite's eyes which widened. Well, well, well! All this beautiful religious equipment just stuck out here in the very back of beyond in this yokel's backyard.

But Micah didn't give him time to mutter more than a "Very fine, isn't it?" before he turned to him again. "Listen. How would you like to stay here and be my priest? Be our family priest? I could pay you ten pieces of silver a year, a complete new suit of clothes and your keep. What do you think?"

What did he think? What would any young out-of-work cleric think in a case like that? It was the chance of a lifetime. He was made.

And so Micah installed the Levite as his family priest, and as he went about his farming and general work about the place, Micah was in a state of near-ecstasy. "Now I know God will make me prosper," he said to himself. "Now that I have a real Levite as my priest, God will certainly help me."

And if this were a "they all lived happily ever after" story, that would be that.

But it is not. It is certainly not that. For something else was happening down in the south, something different altogether.

It was the Danites. They were moving at last. After long, long years of restraint and homelessness they had finally decided to move. And their first action was to appoint five picked men to go as a reconnaissance party and find a suitable spot to settle in.

Northward moved the five scouts, peering and prying into

every valley and gully and hospitable piece of countryside
they passed through. And as they strolled along a winding
mountain track up in the Ephraim hill country one afternoon, sure enough, they came to Micah's place.

"Good afternoon, gentlemen. Strangers here?"

"Yes, we're Danites. Just passing through on our way
north."

"Well, what about stopping for a meal? You must be dry
and hungry. Like to spend the night here? You're very
welcome."

Micah's simple and sincere offer of hospitality was very
acceptable you may be sure, and there they all were, enjoy-
ing a shower and a shave and a nice cool drink. The sun
was just setting when one of them held up his hand for
silence. "Hey, listen! I know that voice. Listen again! Yes,
I'd bet it is. It's that young priest. It's Jonathan. I'll bet it's
Jonathan."

"My goodness, I think you're right. It's that young Benjamite. I knew he was out of a job. He must be working
here with Micah. I wonder what he does."

"I think you're both right. It's his voice all right. But he's
chanting the Hallel—that's how we know his voice. It's that
odd way he has of saying the 'Hear, O Israel'. Sort of
'Hy-arrr'. Sounds as if he's working here as a priest. He
must have fallen on his feet. Half his luck!"

"You wait here, you fellows. I'll go and have a look. This
sounds quite interesting. I'll be back in a moment."

And, sure enough, it was the very same young Benjamite
priest, the young man Jonathan who had been living in their
own village back home in Dan. As he came round to meet
them, as he shook their hands, it was obvious to them all
that he was just bursting with something to tell them.

"Look! Come and I'll show you. You've never seen anything like it. Talk about being lucky! I'll say I've been lucky.
Here, I'll lead the way."

And there to their open-eyed astonishment, was the shrine
with its two silver idols. "See what I mean? They belong
here, they're Micah's. He owns the whole box of tricks.

Just fancy, a little hill-billy Ephraimite with a private shrine
and two silver gods. And that's not all of it—I'm his priest.
Yes, full-time priest, right on his payroll. Ten pieces of
silver and a new suit every year and my keep? Not bad, is
it? And I'm here just to operate it for him. Boy, am I
lucky!"

"Man, you're more than lucky. You just don't know how
tough things are getting back home. Tough as nails!"

"Sure, Jonathan, you've struck it rich. But listen, what
about doing a small job for us? We're on our way north, looking for a new site for our tribe. We're out doing a recce,
hoping to find something. Something good enough to give
us some decent food and living, but not too strongly defended
for us to be able to knock over. Now what about asking God
for us? You've got all the equipment. I'm sure Micah
wouldn't mind if you did a job for us on the side. How
about it?"

And in due time the message came back—the priest made
his enquiries, and the answer was just right. "Go in peace.
Your mission is in the Lord's hands."

Off they set again, buoyed up now by the confidence and
assurance that Micah's priest had brought them from his
investigations through his shrine and idols. Scouting as they
travelled, mile after mile, until finally they were far up to
the north, away past all previous Israelite habitation.

And there was Laish. Laish, a peaceful little isolated community in a lush, fertile fold in the mountain ranges. Unsus-
pecting, prosperous, far removed from the main coastal
centres and defence of their Sidonian culture, there lay the
city of Laish.

An absolute sitting duck. Just waiting to be captured.
The chance of a very lifetime!

Back they raced, nearly one hundred miles, to tell their
tribespeople the exciting news. As they came bursting into
their village again, as the clamour of welcome joined the
urgency of question, the words just gushed from them.
"Come on, let's go! We've seen the very place for us to
take." "Yes, a most beautiful little bit of fertile land, grow

anything you care to plant in it." "OK, fellows, don't simply stand around. Snap into it, it's ours for the taking." "I'll say it is! Look as if we'll be able to walk right up to them and bowl them over before they even know what's hit them." "Sure, God has heard our prayers at last. It's a straight out gift from Heaven, it's got everything we could ask for."

The excitement and the anticipation and the longing cut the preparation time to nearly nothing. It was only a matter of a very few days and they were on their way. The whole tribal convoy was on its way to Laish, to capture Laish, to their new home. Six hundred men in fighting trim, that was their armed strength. All their old folk and their children and their flocks and herds—everything that they owned went with them, they were on their way, they were going north, they were going to Laish. Straight to Laish. No furtive peering, no careful spying, no leisurely searching. No, straight to Laish, non-stop to Laish.

But not quite non-stop. They are excited, they are impatient, they are in a hurry. But one thing will stop them, and that is the thing at Micah's home.

For they were pressing up through the hill country of Ephraim when the five spies called a halt. They beckoned to the tribal elders and held a hurried roadside conference. "Look. You see that place over there, just past the fir trees? That belongs to a chap called Micah. Just a simple little farmer, nice sort of a fellow, very uncomplicated. But do you know what he's got in his place? You'd never believe it, but in his place he's got an ephod and a teraphim, a graven image and a cast image. And there's a beaut little shrine to keep them in, and he's got a genuine Levite priest working it all. We know, we've seen them. And what's more, they do work. Work like one thing. Well? ... What do you reckon? Do you chaps think what we're thinking? OK? Come on, let's go!"

The party came to a noisy, chatter-filled stop at the front gate. Six hundred men not making any particular attempt to be quiet are hard to miss. The most devout priest in all the world is likely to have his devotions considerably disturbed

by a crowd like that, and Micah's Levite was no particular
exception. Out he came to meet them, and what a hand-
shaking and a general how-de-do all round. And in the middle
of it, as he was completely bewildered and bustled by the
reunion, he just happened to glance out the corner of his
left eye. And there they were, right in the very process of
decamping with all his religious gear. Ephod, teraphim,
graven image, cast image—the lost—the whole shrineful.
Just nipping over the back fence and dashing off to the main
road. There to his utter dismay, went all his box of tricks.

Jonathan leaped to his feet from the big log he had been
squatting on as he yarned with his old neighbours. A great
bellowing shout of rage burst out of him. "Hey! Stop! What
are you doing? Wait! You dirty sneaks, put those back!
Hey! Stop!"

But the cries died away. Died suddenly. Died the very
instant that he saw the few large fists clenched tightly right
in front of his face. Knuckles shining white under the skin,
fists that moved slowly, menacingly, just a few inches from
his teeth!

"Shut up, d'you hear? Keep your big mouth shut, or
else! Now listen, buster, and here's your really big chance
to do yourself a whole lot of good. Just look at it like this:
here we are, a whole tribe, see? Well, why not say you'll
join us as our priest? Eh? That's quite a something for a
young fellow like you. I'll say it is! Join us, that's what
we're saying."

"Yes, young Jonathan, think again. It's not really right,
is it? You being a priest just to one man when we're a
whole tribe and we haven't got one? See? Far better in
every way if you were with us instead of this farmer chap
out here in the back of beyond. Well, what do you think?"

What did he think? What did he say? Just what would
any young parson say, three thousand years ago in the hill
country of Ephraim, or right here in twentieth-century
Sydney? Curate in some remote little home mission parish,
or diocesan bishop? Priest to a whole tribe, instead of to a
single isolated family?

It's not a question at all, is it? It's really a simple state-ment of what is going to happen. There was no king in Israel, remember, every man did what was right in his own eyes. And there was mighty little guidance needed to per-suade the priest as to what was right in a simple matter like this.

"This pleased the priest, so he took the ephod and tera-phim, the idol and the image, and joined the company."

Yes, it was pretty easy for that itinerant, homeless, Levi-tical priest to decide what was right. But what *he* said was right was certainly not what Micah said was right.

For the Danites were hardly down the road more than a few hundred yards before Micah came home and saw his staggering loss. Gone, all gone! Gods, shrine, priest and all —gone!

"My gods! My shrine! They're gone! They've been stolen! Boy, quick, dash off and tell the neighbours and collect them up. Hurry, we'll catch up with them and have it out. The dirty sneaks! Stealing my gods, the gods I made myself, and my shrine and my priest too! The lousy cheat-ing crooks! Come on, men, grab a good stout cudgel and let's catch them."

No trouble catching up with them. The trouble starts when you do catch up with them. For the Danites had moved their women and children and flocks out to the front and had all the six hundred fighting men in strong defensive formation at the rear.

Poor Micah hadn't really noticed this. He was too much disturbed to notice little practicalities like that. As he came dashing up with his small band of retainers, calling "Stop! Stop!" and "Hey! Wait for us!" it all came to a very sudden halt.

The Danites turned and faced him. "What's the matter, buster? What's all that crowd with you for? Who's that you've got following you? Yes, tell us your little troubles."

Micah was still puffing and panting from his running, and still hadn't really noticed the essential politics of this direct confrontation technique that he had adopted.

His words tumbled out, hot and bitter. "Well, of all the cool cheek! You come and just steal my gods—gods I actually made myself, my own personal property—and take away my priest. And then you ask me what's the matter!"

One of the Danites—one of the biggest, probably one of the front-row forwards in the tribal Rugby team—stepped forward and jutted his chin right up in front of Micah's face, and spoke slowly and quietly. "Listen, mate, you ought to be more careful. You talk a bit too loud, see? Somebody might hear you some day, talking like that. That's not too good, see? It might annoy some of the fellows. They're easily upset, see, and it'd be a pity for you then. They'd tear you right apart. Chew you up into little pieces. That's what they'd do. They'd snuff you out just as quickly as you could count one-two!" And he raised his voice a little, without lifting his head, breathing all over Micah as he almost bellowed: "And that goes for the rest of this bunch of runts, too. They'd stouch the whole stupid lot of you. Now you'd better shut that big mouth of yours and keep it shut!" He stepped back a couple of paces and stared hard and coldly into Micah's now whitened face. "D'you get me, mister? Compre? Then scram!"

"With that the Danites went on their way and Micah, seeing that they were too strong for him, turned and went home.

"Thus they carried off the priest and the things Micah had made for himself, and attacked Laish, whose people were quiet and carefree. They put them to the sword and set fire to their city. There was no one to save them, for the city was a long way from Sidon and they had no contact with the Aramaeans, although the city was in the vale near Beth-rehob. They rebuilt the city and settled in it, naming it Dan after the name of their forefather Dan, a son of Israel; but its original name was Laish. The Danites set up the idol, and Jonathan son of Gershom, son of Moses, and his sons were priests to the tribe of Dan until the people went into exile. (They set

up for themselves the idol which Micah had made, and
it was there as long as the house of God was at Shiloh.)
"In those days when no king ruled in Israel ..."

This is the second story ...
I don't know his name. All that we are told is that he
was a Levite, and that he "was living in the heart of the
hill country of Ephraim". Whether he lived there perma-
nently or worked there or was just there on a holiday, your
guess is as good as anybody else's.

But whatever he was doing, he was not doing it alone.
For he had his wife with him. At least, she was a slave-wife,
which rather suggests that he had another wife of higher
social status hidden away somewhere, but even that is only
a guess—no other woman comes into this story in any personal way, and the concubine (slave-wife) is the wife we
are concerned with. For it was she who started it all going.
She walked out on him. Just up and went home. Not home
to mum, but home to dad. And dad lived in Benjamin.

And after four months without her, the Levite decided
to go after her; so he followed her down to dad's place in
Benjamin. He took a servant with him and a couple of asses
for transport.

Now this story would make no end of a teaser as a study
in marriage relationships, but that is not the thing I am
looking at. Indeed, the relationships are so topsy-turvy that
it would be hard to say just what were the motives for much
that happened—but that is by the way. For dad did not
meet him with the traditional shotgun, dad met him with
open arms and warm hospitality and lots to eat and lots to
drink. They were real buddies, and I must confess that the
girl was somewhat overlooked in the general run of festivities. I still can't understand how the daughter could be a
slave, when dad seems so well heeled, at any rate so far as
food and grog indicate the state of his exchequer.

But the welcome was cordial and the beano was quite a
party. Quite a party! For it was four days before they began
to thaw out enough to start remembering what it was all

about. And on the fourth day the Levite said to his father-in-law, "Well, thanks for a jolly good time. I hope I can return the hospitality. Any time you should be passing through our desolate bit of country, drop in, and I'll try and make it up to you. Thanks a million, and we'll be on our way."

So the morning of the fourth day dawned bright and clear, and the Levite and his wife packed up and saddled their asses for their departure. But dad met them before they got in the saddles, and would not hear a word of it. "But, my dear boy, you simply can't go like this. You must stay and have a bit of a snack. You can't tackle the long journey home without a good square meal. Now then, come along in and sit down. A good hearty breakfast is just the thing for a long trip."

"So the two of them sat down and ate and drank together." And the sitting and the eating and the drinking seemed to go on right through the day, because it was evening before the Levite woke up to the fact that he hadn't got going at all, that the day was in fact over. And father-in-law was very insistent that they should stay the night again, and there they were on the fifth day.

And again they got into the saddles and were just about to push off for the out-back, when the old man turned up and repeated his argument about the need of a good sound meal. I must say that I think this old Benjamite was the ultimate in big-hearted hospitality. So that again they dismounted and again they sat down to some good solid tucker. The day wore on, the food and the drink were on a par, it was another day of good cheer.

And as evening began to close in, as the shadows lengthened and the sky crimsoned in the west, the father-in-law invited them to stay the night yet a sixth time.

But this time the priest was adamant. I can't for the life of me think how this man's mind ticked, but at last he dug his toes in and just refused to stay any longer. In spite of his father-in-law's pleas and arguments about the day being as good as done and why take a risk by travelling at night and so on and so on, he wouldn't hear of it. "No, thanks again for your kindness, but I must be going this time."

"But it's nearly night-time, why not stop overnight and get away first thing in the morning? That would be so much easier and safer."

But no, the Levite refused point-blank. And so there they were at last, out on the road north as the night began to close in around them. I often wonder how it would have fared for the whole history of their people if that Levite had stayed just that one more night. For as they travelled into the dusk, it soon became obvious that they would have to find somewhere to stop over for the night. It was getting dark, long past the time for people to be travelling those tortuous unpaved mountain tracks. It was dangerous now, and extremely difficult. But the Levite seemed clear on one thing at least, and that was that he wanted to get clean away from his Benjamite father-in-law.

I don't think the servant's strength was failing, I think it's more likely that his nerve was failing. "Sir," he said at last, and it was nearly dark, "sir, what about Jebus? That's Jebus just over there on the top of the next rise. We could easily go there for the night, it's a real slap-up city, and we'd have no trouble getting lodging there overnight."

What the wife thought of this suggestion we do not know. What she thought of anything at all, we really do not know —she was just a slave-wife, the poor thing, and she didn't seem to count at all.

But what the Levite thought of the idea we do know. He thought it stank! Thumbs down! "Great Scott, man, what an idea! Foreigners. Spend the night with foreigners? Wouldn't dream of it! I'm shocked at the very idea. No Israelites there at all, it's a wretched heathen hide-out if ever there was. No, come on, we'll go to Gibeah. Either Gibeah or Ramah. We'll go to one of our own towns, but certainly not to Jebus!"

And I can't help the wry smile that twists the corners of my mouth at this so-human incident of over three thousand years ago. I think of how many times history has been re-shaped by just this very same thing: the catholic-protestant distrust, the high-low Church conflict, the establishment-dissenter bitterness, even the Jews having no dealings with the Samaritans in the time of Christ—this is the human contrariness that makes such a mirthless smile as I see the tug on the reins and the flick of the whip as that Levite swung his donkey's head away from Jebus.

But the smile that is on my face is certainly not on the faces of the travellers. For it is now night, the sun has completely disappeared, only the stars give the light that guides their sure-footed mounts as they pick out the faint pallor that distinguishes the road from the night.

But at last it's over, the all-Israelite town of Gibeah is ahead, no problem now with foreigners and false religions and all such unhealthy dangers. They've reached Gibeah, Gibeah in Benjamin.

And I admit freely that I'm not smiling now. Neither is the Levite, however glad he may be that as a good, respectable priest he has done the correct thing. And neither is his servant. And there is certainly no smile on the face of the poor wife, for whom there is never again to be a smile at all. Gibeah after sunset is not the place to bring out a smile on the face of anybody!

For the place is in darkness. Every door shut, not a soul to be seen, the little square in the middle of the town is completely deserted. Gibeah in Benjamin.

So that there was nothing else to do. As their donkeys clip-clopped noisily on the pavement, there was no other sound to be heard at all; yet they still knew that they were heard. Only the tiniest glimmer of light showed in the chinks of doors and windows that were all tight-shut—but they knew that they were seen. Heard by hidden ears, watched by unseen eyes. Gibeah.

No door opened, no window raised. No voice to greet them, no guide to show them to a warm and sheltered lodging. No, nothing like that. They just sat down to spend the night in the loneliness of the city square. Gibeah, Gibeah in Benjamin.

Yes, this was Gibeah of Benjamin. Not hated Jebus. No

foreign power ruling here, just the tiny stronghold of the Benjamites themselves, the people of God, the light of the world. Gibeah!

How long they may have stayed there, sitting cold and lonely in the middle of the tiny cobbled square, you may guess and I may guess. Only Gibeah itself could ever tell us that answer. But as the night wore on and the hour grew late, in through the city gate came a bent old man, feet shuffling wearily after an over-long day of toiling in the fields outside. As the pale starlight showed him the shadowed shadows that was all he could see of the huddled strangers, he came over to them. "Good evening, but can I help you? Are you leaving the town? Or are you just arriving? Do you need help?"

"No, thank you," said the Levite. "We are strangers here. We have been down in Bethlehem, in Judah, and are on our way to my home in the hill country of Ephraim. But this seems to be a very quiet town. Nobody has opened a single door since we arrived, we haven't seen a soul. It's a strange place, we're beginning to think. Not that we need help—we have food and drink and fodder for the asses. We're not short of anything, really."

"Well," said the old farmer, "I'm from the hill country of Ephraim, too, I'm only staying here for a short time. But you must come home with me. I couldn't possibly leave you here out in the middle of the town square."

"Thank you for your kind offer, but we will be quite all right. We are pretty comfortable, really, and it's only a stop-over halt for us. This is a very quiet town, and we'll be off in the morning."

"Oh, no!" The old man's words were sharp and emphatic. There was an urgency that seemed out of all proportion to the event. "Please, come home with me and spend the night at my place. That's the least I can do."

I think that the Levite was glad to have a companion, even an old labouring man, from the hill country of his own background. I think that. I also imagine that the servant was only too glad to exchange the village cobblestones for something more soft and comfortable in the way of bedding. I feel that I am right in imagining that. But the wife, the poor wife who had run away from home, slave-wife that she was and a mere chattel that could be bought and sold—I'm altogether sure that she was glad to be inside good solid doors and walls. To have plenty of light instead of the fitful starlight in the village square. To have the comfort of hearing the men in the next room, as they now sat and yawned and drank together, the clink of glasses and the gloggle-gloggle of wine poured freely, the burst of laughter from some ribald reminiscence of the days in the hill country of Ephraim— all of this taking her into a quiet restful sleep. Yes, I'm sure the wife felt that, felt glad of the chance that had brought them here for the night. Here to Gibeah, Gibeah in Benjamin.

And now I'm wondering about something else. Hmm, it's all really a bit quaint and I suppose there's some reason why nobody has opened a single door to say goodnight to the Levite and his wife, maybe they're only minding their own business and it's very quiet and peaceful now, just the low rumble of the two men's voices to be heard as the others are all asleep in the house and I think I can slip off myself. There's nothing likely to happen now in Gibeah in Benjamin ...

Bang! It is a boot. A boot kicking on a door. "Hey! Open up, there!" "Yes, come on. Open that door before we kick it in!" And the kick is repeated, louder, heavier, this time, and fists begin to pound a belabouring demand as voices begin to call out. Loud voices. Men's voices!

And now there is a hand on the latch, a strong, angry hand that is shaking the door as if to rip the very hinges out of the jamb. "Now then, you old rotter, you know what we want." "Sure, it's that fellow with you. It's him we want." "Come on, open up! We want our bit of fun, can you hear, and we want him." "Say, you'd better open that door before we tear the place to pieces."

It is Gibeah. The whole square is now thundering with the heavy bellowing clamour of voices, male voices, the rising pitch monitoring the rising passions, the shouts and the bangs being joined by the heavy tread of added feet as others come to join the orgy.

It is not bestial—beasts don't suffer perversions like this. It is not devilish—devils don't have hormones. It is just human—it's men. Men of Gibeah, Gibeah in Benjamin.

No wonder the historian is so upset. No wonder he is so bewildered, as he sets out to write this shocking story. It's not "once upon a time", it's "in those days there was no king in Israel". It's the time when it may truly be said, "If the only light you have is darkness, the darkness is doubly dark." Yes, God is warning, if there is no king in Israel, then each man of faith will still do what he thinks to be right. But if there is no king in Israel, *and* there is no man of faith at all—it is indeed darkness that is doubly dark!

It is Gibeah.

"No! No! Please! Listen, you men, listen to me!" It's the poor old farmer, visitor himself in their city, who is replying. His voice is shaking, his age and his distress and his fear all mingled in growing horror at the dreadful predicament confronting him. "Men! Please! You can't do such a shameful thing. This man is a visitor, he's my guest, what you're planning is vile and hideous!"

But human passion knows no shame as it knows no respect. The poor old man was at breaking-point. "Look, I've got a daughter, she's a virgin, I'd rather give her to you. His slave-wife is here—why not have her? But not a man who is my guest."

No shame. No regret. Not in Gibeah.

Until finally the old man lost his own sense of shame as he lost even his self-respect. It was the slave-wife he grabbed, the poor woman who had already seen such bitter tragedy, the human chattel that had been up for sale to the highest bidder—she it was whom he seized. Out into the dead of night, out into the mauling lust of the passion-driven men of Gibeah, the poor creature was tossed. Hour after hour, until dawn began to break, she was their bait, their game, their sport. Only the greying in the eastern sky, the first blush of light which frightens away such men of darkness, ended her agony, as at last she fell helplessly and piteously at the door of the old Ephraimite's home.

And when her husband arose in the morning, intent on getting away, there lay his wife on the doorstep. "Come on," he said impatiently, "you'd better get moving. Come on, we must go."

"But there was no answer." That is how the Old Testament writer says it. I am sure that I can still feel, over three thousand years later, the thing that the historian himself felt, as he simply recorded this story. "But there was no answer." There was no answer, there is no answer, there will be no answer. Past, present and future, in tense as in fact, there's nothing more to say. Death like that, sheer pitch-black evil like that, are altogether unanswerable.

I don't know what you would do if it had been your experience. I don't know what I should have done if it had been mine. But I do know what that Levite did. He picked up the body of his wife and put it on his donkey. And he went home, right back to the hills of Ephraim. And he took her off his ass. And he cut her body into twelve pieces, limb by limb. And he despatched the ghastly pieces through the length and breadth of Israel. That's what he did.

There was no king in Israel. No, but there was a tiny bit of conscience left, at any rate in the other tribes. Not in Benjamin of course. In Benjamin darkness was now serving as light, and there was no king and no conscience.

As the grisly, corrupting pieces of human limb and flesh went north and south, east and west through the whole of the little country, there arose a concern and a resentment such as had never before stirred all Israel. Down to Mizpah, to the watchtower, streamed the whole congregation of the people, every elder and chief and able-bodied fighting man of all the assembly of the nation, stirred to prayer and action by this sombre, shameful challenge.

As the husband of the murdered woman told the huge concourse of men about the abomination and the wantonness that Gibeah expressed in the very heart of their nation, the response was unanimous: "Not one of us shall go back to his tent, not one of us shall return home." That was the motion that was carried unanimously. They would never face home or family or God again if evil like this was not punished.

Down to Benjamin, to the tribal leaders, went the curt command: "What is this wicked thing which has happened in your midst? Hand over to us those scoundrels in Gibeah, and we will put them to death and purge Israel of this wickedness." It was a command, but it was equally a rebuke. And all Benjamin, leaders and men alike, scoffed at the command and sneered at the rebuke.

It was war. Civil war. All Israel *v.* Benjamin. Yes, it was civil war; but it was also light *v.* darkness, good *v.* evil.

Judah, the tribe of Judah, drew the lot that was cast for the privilege of attacking first. Judah was the neighbour tribe to Benjamin, Judah was the tribe that should have known most about the sordid affairs of Benjamin. And I can't help wondering whether something that was the black soul of Benjamin had not rubbed off on Judah. I can only guess, and so must you. But no doubt at all God knew. And Judah got thrashed. The Benjamites had a special unit, a band of seven hundred small-arms men of brilliant skill and strategy. Slingers, men who could "sling a stone and not miss by a hair's breadth". Crack-shots, experts, these seven hundred were all left-handers, they were all killers. And they were all from Gibeah!

There was a grim council of war that night. Defeat, when they were doing what they thought was right. No king, for sure, in Israel, but should not men indeed do what they think is right?

Of course they should! And the next day they attacked again, this time *en masse*.

And down they went again, that murderous hail of sling-hurled missiles cracking skulls and breaking bones with frightening accuracy and deadliness.

And this time the council of war was much more subdued. This time it was at Bethel that they met. And this time they met to pray, to offer sacrifice, to weep, even, as in deep repentance they implored the help and advice of God. The ark of the covenant was at Bethel, Phineas was there, the Phineas who was a direct descendant of Aaron their original High Priest under Moses. And God was at Bethel. As they asked the advice and council of Phineas, as he sought the clear direction of God, the answer came: "Attack him: tomorrow I will deliver him into your hands."

It is said of the early Church that the first-century Christians out-lived, out-died and out-thought the pagan Roman world around them. And this is as true of light overcoming darkness in the early Christian era as it was a thousand years before that time, as it must be now, two thousand years later.

And Israel did just that. No hope of out-living the Benjamites, useless in out-dying them, if they could not out-think them. This time the strategy was that of God, the plan of attack was not merely the product of bitter remorse.

For down to battle came Israel, this time prepared to die, determined to live, but beginning to think. As they came into open, head-on clash, out poured the Benjamites again, their sling-and-stone machine-guns blazing, the heady flavour of two previous days of victory tickling their military palate most encouragingly. And back and back retreated the Israelites, yielding first yard after yard, finally mile after mile. And it looked to the advancing Benjamites as though it were again all over, it seemed that again light had to yield to darkness, evil had triumphed over good.

Then suddenly something changed. The retreating Israelites rallied, stiffened their lines of battle, and this time Benjamin had to pause, even yield a step. And as they did so, as they looked back for that moment in which to make the short retreat, they saw it. There, behind them, was the whole sky black with smoke! Smoke from their burning city. Gibeah, ablaze!

For the Israelites had sent a small ambush party round in a secret flanking movement and had captured and now destroyed the Benjamin headquarters. Gibeah was an inferno, the smoke and glare filled the whole sky—Benjamin was now trapped in the jaws of the pincer.

It was a massacre—killed in battle, mowed down on the roads as they fled, pursued far into the wilderness, the tribe was almost annihilated. Only six hundred men escaped, escaped by fleeing far out towards the desert, away out to the loneliness of the Rock of Rimmon—men who were as good as dead! Cut off from their people, no women to bear them children, the whole story of the tribe of Benjamin was virtually at an end. The nation that had been twelve tribes was now to be eleven.

And that was what the others began to see. Out there in the desert, living grimly as men in a desert may alone live, the six hundred were all of Benjamin that was left. Every other man, woman and child gone—wiped out! And now the elders of all the rest of Israel began to realise this. Eleven, where there had always been twelve. Benjamin gone. Eleven, not twelve.

Until finally Israel was in mourning again. The bitter tears that they had wept for the evil life of Benjamin became still more bitter for the awful death of Benjamin. Prayer, sacrifice, anguish—these were their weapons now, fighting this time to defend the life of the tribe they had so nearly destroyed. And there was nothing they could do, for they had sworn a solemn oath that no single one of them would allow his daughter to marry a Benjamite. Nothing now that they could do.

Yes, they were all involved. They had all entered into the pledge together, no dissentients, not a single "no", not even one "abstain from voting". Unanimous.

And then somebody began to count, began to tick off names and places—and came up with the exciting discovery that Jabesh-Gilead was not there. Not a single representative from the Jabesh sub-county in Gilead. Jabesh-Gilead had not made any promise, it was bound by no covenant, no solemn oath had passed over Jabesh lips.

And the hot feeling of resentment against Jabesh, for failing to come to the attack on Benjamin, was now coupled with a splendid solution to their dilemma!

Quickly a commando group was assembled, top-rating assault troops, this time to attack Jabesh. Not just to attack the men, as in Gibeah, but this time to capture the girls. The girls of Jabesh were the booty, all the non-mated, adolescent and sub-adolescent girls were to be brought in. And all the other people, men, women and children were to be killed! Jabesh would pay dearly for its refusal to come to the attack on Benjamin, paying not only with her life, but also with her daughters.

It was a lightning raid that caught the local Gileadites completely by surprise. Four hundred single girls made up the prize that they carried off, all that was left of Jabesh-Gilead.

And so the message was despatched to the six hundred Benjamites out by the Rock of Rimmon. The message of peace, of hope, of forgiveness. And the four hundred maids were handed over to the six hundred Benjamite survivors, to re-populate and so rebuild the tribe. The tribes were still twelve. The darkness had not overwhelmed the light.

And I am feeling terrible. The whole thing, from the moment when the poor little concubine ran away from her husband to go back to her home in Benjamin, to her shocking death in the streets of Gibeah, to this monstrous event in which a whole village is entirely wiped out to provide women for men who seem so unworthy of life at all—the whole ghastly tale is frightening and sickening. And I wonder just what will come out of all this? What hope is there, in a proper emotional sense, for children born to these women in such loveless mating, what psychological hazards will this be throwing into the whole social matrix? Yes, I ask, what of all this? And what, further, of the precarious instability of a society of four hundred women handed over to six hundred men?

And even as I say this, even as I start to think this, I find that it's not even told yet. For the elders of Israel have been asking the very same questions. Four hundred divided into six hundred won't go. What, then, can be done?

And up came the answer. Why, what about the girls at

Shiloh? Yes, plenty of girls at Shiloh! Why not take a couple of hundred of them? Yes, get the girls at Shiloh.

For Shiloh was the second principal sanctuary of the whole of Israel, the ark of the covenant was either at Shiloh or at nearby Bethel. Shiloh was a very important religious centre.

But that was not what the men were thinking about. They were remembering that there was some rather fancy dancing at the annual festival at Shiloh, and there was a more than even chance that the single girls would put on a dance!

"Now," they said, "we can't give our daughters to the Benjamites, we have sworn a solemn oath against it. In fact we've put a curse on any man who gives his daughter in marriage to a Benjamite, and curses are terribly powerful things. But listen, you Benjamites, you two hundred men who didn't manage to get a girl from Jabesh, if you like to go up to Shiloh and hide among the vines around the dancing area, and if the girls do come out to dance, then there's your chance. Grab a girl, and she's yours! And if the girl's family protest and kick up a fuss, they'll be sure to come and complain to us. Then we will say, 'Please hand the girl over in good grace, because we didn't take her in battle as a captive—that would never do, of course—and we didn't ask you to give her to the man voluntarily, as that would be to incur the guilt of the solemn vow.' Now, then, what about that? You should be able to get a wife apiece at Shiloh."

And it is in fact with this miserable bit of cheating and lying and thuggery and superstition that the tale is concluded. That is the end of the story. For as the men of Benjamin came to Shiloh, as the girls came out to dance and rejoice, the men sprang in. A girl apiece was the arrangement, and that was the way it worked out. The sad, desperate record of the blackness of Benjamin is told. "In those days there was no king in Israel and every man did what was right in his own eyes."

EPILOGUE

"In a sense we are lost, for we do drift about in rough and uncharted seas. We are fearful that if we do establish a steady course it may take us somewhere we do not want to go. We also know that the huge waves tossed up from the depths of conservative tradition and State authority may weaken or even destroy us." So wrote Dale A. Johnson from his teaching desk at the University of California. And so would say teachers and students alike in many a centre if they were only willing and articulate enough to put their thoughts into words.

For the simple truth is that there are countless men in this sophisticated western world who share this sense of being utterly lost. Myriads, there are, who see life as being completely meaningless and pointless, a mere biological existence in which the naked ape that is *homo sapiens* is now the central figure of doom.

That is what I wrote at the very beginning of this book. And I wonder whether this is not really much the same thing, in our twentieth century, that the writer of the Book of Judges was saying in his time: "In those days there was no king ..." And I ask myself, can it be true again? Is there still no king?

But can I be sure that I am detached enough, uninvolved enough, to gain sufficient objectivity to make a proper judgment? The player in the middle of the football scrum knows full well how tough the game may be—but is he the man to describe the detail and the tactics of the match?

So that in my imagination I see a science-fiction visitor from outer space come and touch down on this little planet; come here to give his account of man today. I wonder what he will record. Yes, I wonder deeply ...

As his sensitive antenna tunes in to the spiritual wave-length of human experience, what, indeed, will he find? As he programmes all this detail into his astro-computer, will the outcoming signal read: *There is no king*? As he moves from his study of the spirit-worship and animism of so many "primitive" peoples; to the strength-sapping, soul-destroying pantheism of the eastern mystics; to the power-less ethic of the Buddha and the Ancestors; to the heartless fatalism of Islam; to the orderless conglomeration of Christendom itself—yes, what will his answer be? Still: *No king*? Plenty of priests, of course. Levites galore. No shortage of religion, man-made ideas and superstitions in myriad array—yes, but no king.

And I wonder further, as I see his searchings begin to probe yet deeper still into the very mind and soul of this sophisticated Christendom. Yes, I wonder much more. This western world whose whole economy survives only because of its sheer extravagant gluttony; that has as its stock-in-trade an utter devotion to war-planning aggression; that expresses its wanton pride in hurling vast extravagances into the uselessness of space; that is quite content to sit and watch the majority of other men starve piteously to death; that spends hour after hour, night after night, viewing count-less screens where lust is shown as love and adultery is regarded as success and chastity is a funny word and even the deeply personal tragedy of impotence can become wide-screen 70-mm mass-entertainment comedy—sure, I don't need to guess what a mere space-traveller would say, I can begin to tell his answers for him: *There must indeed be no king in the planet earth.*

No, I no longer need that visitor to earth to tell me these answers, I am beginning to make my own replies. I simply cannot mistake them.

As I flip the pages of the daily newspapers and thumb through the weeklies and digests and journals, as I twiddle the knobs of my transistor and click from channel to channel of the T.V.: no sound or sight of a king. All the opinions in the world, advice ladled out by the bucket, man-made policy and human judgment no end—but no king. Still no king.

Religion—yes, still plenty of religion in this space-occupying world of ours. But religion that has been discounted, religion that has become a joke, religion that has even filled many men's hearts with hate. Sure, there is no end to our religion, we wonder if it's not still our biggest single business, even. But that's the trouble, it just seems to be our biggest business. But where is the king? Is there indeed a king? No king?

And yet, I keep saying, God is *God*. This is still His world, the purposes of Heaven are still being lived out in the life-to-death struggle of humans. God is altogether God. The tough, bitter, crude experiences of over thirty centuries ago in the land of the Judges may still be rediscovered in the sophisticated, disillusioned, veneered sham that is the vaunted wealth of this late twentieth century of ours. There they are, still to be found, a humble Barak, a brilliant Gideon, a sad and lonely Jephthah, or even the man who is bursting in reactionary conflict like Samson—but men of faith. Just a few. Perhaps a very few. But some. Naked apes like the rest of men, but the naked ape that is a man who says simply and honestly: "My hand is in the hand of God. I belong to God."

That is faith. That is real faith. That is the relationship that man may experience with his God. Not a matter of genuflecting at the appropriate moment in the liturgy, not even a matter of having a precise and accurate knowledge of the Greek and Hebrew of the Bible text. Just that intention to belong to God.

And that is what this extraordinary old book out of the past has been saying. Not in words of philosophical debate or theological argumentation—it is quite remarkably free of all such reading matter. But told in the activities and affairs of men and women going about their searching, challenging, dangerous tasks as humans.

And even if in these modern days there seems to be no king, it is still altogether true that this is God's world, for always God is *God*. Yes, there are in fact the few who know the king, even today. Like Barak and Gideon, in company with Jephthah and Samson, there are the people who have heard the call of God, they now belong to Him.

For the king is none other than Jesus of Nazareth, the Christ. They work for Him. They live for Him. Truly, they belong to Him. If you meet them you wouldn't know, perhaps, because they are so ordinary and everyday and human. But when you probe more deeply, find their motives, their goals, their purposes, then it is that you discover the truth —they are men of God. They know God. They do know the king.

I meet them. I talk to them ...

One is a physicist, world leader in his exalted speciality; and when I meet him he is busy daubing *Araldite* on the beautiful little piece of instrumentation that he is going to rocket on to the surface of Mars. Sir, I ask, anxiously, eagerly, you say you know the king? Did you discover him with that last space probe you launched at Woomera? Or at Cape Kennedy? Is that the way you found the king?

"John Hercus," he replies, "I found the king on earth, not on Mars, any more than I found him on the moon. He is here. I've been in conference with him today. The king is the living Christ Himself! God was in Christ reconciling the world to Himself is how Saint Paul explains the historical phenomenon of Jesus of Nazareth. I met Him today, will meet Him again and again today and every day."

And you, sir? I ask, turning to another. You say you know the king? You are also a scientist, but you are world-famous for your knowledge of evolution, not of the physics of outer space. Did you meet the king in all those fossils you know so much about? Meet him in all those millions of years of life and death that make up the biological story of this planet?

"Yes," he replies, "I did indeed meet the king in the story of life and of death. But it was the life and the death of Christ. It is in the person of Jesus, Who lived and Who died and Who now lives an altogether new kind of life, that I have learned the real meaning of all other life and death. It is His life that I am now seeking to live, not just the life of a palaeontologist."

And so I could go on, for so in fact I do go on. One here, another there. The over-busy housewife with the cares and responsibilities of the fast-growing family and the slow-growing purse—how simply and how seriously she tells me of her day-to-day encounter with the king. The student, the labourer, the top executive and his least-paid typist in his biggest office, the theologian—yes, there are a few of them, too—the teacher, the bricklayer, the farmer. Only a handful, really, but all saying the same: "I know the king."

Not a vast throng, nothing like the crowd that is packed into the sports arena; but the ones and the twos that still make up the total of the family of God. Some knowing a great deal about God, some knowing very little. But all knowing this one thing: I know *Him*.

And now perhaps you see it as I saw it myself and still keep seeing it.

For this is where I came in. This is exactly where I came in. God is *God*. The king is in fact here, right here all the time. Untrusted by business, unrecognised by leisure, unserved by science and education, unhonoured by great masters of modern religion—but God, just the same.

In intention, that is precisely what this book has been saying, because that is precisely what I think God has always been saying. This is His world and He is working out His purposes in the lives and affairs of men and women in His world.

I believe that this is true of the world today, just as true as ever it was in the days of those men I met in the Book of Judges. I think this is true of the President in the White House just as much as it is true of the humblest wretch who was ever caught up in the foulness of Vietnam or Korea or even the trenches of Flanders. And I think it is true of my life, too, as it is true of the people I meet all day in the encounter of modern medical practice. For whether President or G.I., doctor or patient, that is just the setting in which God has put us, merely the machinery He is using, as He probes our deepest being with His searching will. And yes, I am sure that this is true, true of you, too.

This is certainly what I saw in the Book of Judges. In the excitement and the pathos and the rising drama of this so-disturbing old Hebrew record, this is simply bursting out of every page. I don't think these stories are showing mere chance, mere luck, a mere spin of a mechanistic coin as impersonal machinery runs its unplanned, self-determining course. You may think that. So may a lot of other people. —but not John Hercus. I do not think that. I don't think that about Samson or about Jephthah or about Gideon or Barak, and I don't even think that about Ehud and his dagger. Because I don't think that about Jesus, the man God became, living right here in the very middle of history nearly two thousand years ago. No, I don't think that about Jesus Christ, I do not think He just "happened" as a rather unusual specimen of the human variant in biological evolution. You might, but I don't. And that is why I don't think it of the men in the Book of Judges.

Let me make this quite clear, please: these stories we have been looking at make sense to me, Heaven-sized sense, because of what I know of Christ; I certainly do not think He makes sense just because of them. I think those men were alive on this little planet, alongside you and me and the rest of us, only because of Christ. And I don't imagine for one moment that He had to come to earth to patch up some problem blundering humans had brought about.

And I can see the glint of eye and curl of lip as someone says, "Ha. John Hercus, you'd better be careful. Because you haven't forgotten Dan and Benjamin, have you? What about that story? Is God still God, or has He just forgotten all about it?"

No, I have not forgotten. How could I ever forget a story like that?

For I believe that in the account of Micah and Jonathan and the tribe of Dan, even in that story, there were some, some at least, who were doing the thing that seemed right in their own eyes. Jonathan was doing that, strange though it may seem. That sheer opportunism that took him travelling round the hill country of Ephraim, picking up a job now with Micah, now with the tribe of Dan, was not the cheap thing that was expediency, it was really faith. He thought he was doing the thing that God wanted, he thought that this was indeed the call of God. I may not have thought so, you may not think so even yet; but, God is saying, *He* thought so! All these odd happenings "pleased the priest", God records, the priest was at peace with God, he was doing what seemed right in his own eyes. I am guessing now, but I think that this was true of Micah's mother also. I think that she was in fact following the meagre glimmer of truth that managed to enlighten her spirit in the middle of all that hill country gloom. All that jazz about "cursing" and "blessing", just so much superstitious mumbo-jumbo to you and to me, no doubt, was to her the absolute truth—and she followed the truth she knew. You know better truth than that, surely. I know better truth than that, certainly, for I have met the One Who *is* Truth. But that is our great privilege. She just did what she thought was right. And I'm guessing again, I know, but I think the same about Micah himself. Sure, God doesn't say so, but Micah does, and I'm happy to take his word for it. "I know that the Lord will make me prosper, because I have a Levite for my priest," Micah said. He certainly thought he was doing what was right, however absurd it may seem to you or to me.

Yes, I think I am reading that story correctly. No king, dear me, no, nothing in the least little bit like a king; but those few people were doing what they thought was right, they were doing what seemed right in their own eyes. So that if God is indeed *God*, what a wonderful story this is, seen properly, as it tells us of the way God makes His will known to men living in the isolation of ignorance like this. And what a warning, what a graphic warning, to seek the presence of the One Who is Himself the Light of the world. No wonder Jesus stops to warn us so strikingly that if the spiritual sight of the people is so sick, then we must expect to find that even the light may appear to be pretty dark.

"But what about Benjamin?" And now I can't miss either the taunt or the sneer as the answer flashes back at me. "Yes, John Hercus, that's all very well for the tribe of Dan and all that deeply rooted superstition. But you've still got Benjamin to explain. How does Gibeah fit in? If God is *God*, really God, what about Gibeah? No King still, but no superstition either. No men of faith at all—what sense does this story make? Does God just forget to be God now and again? Does Gibeah get out of His grasp, can Benjamin get away with anything it likes?"

And I stop to wipe my brow, for a dew has started to form. Not because it is hot, too hot, this lovely late summer day in sunny Sydney, but because of the warmth of the concern that is now distressing me. For I think I do in fact know the answer to that question, and I think the story of Benjamin is telling it to me as never anywhere else in all scripture. And the answer is frightening.

For I remember what happened to Benjamin. I remember the awful death of all Benjamin, a death that was cheated only by the depth of the concern of the other fellow tribesmen. For that was still God at work. That was the altogether awesome thing that is the judgment of God. That was light dispelling darkness. God still God.

And now I remember something else—something that happened in my own world, something that deeply involved my own life. I remember the black darkness that was Hitler, the evil that gathered under the banner of the swastika. Not mere perverted lust, as in Gibeah; but the cold-blooded scientific deadliness that turned a fellow man into the cheapest expendable experimental animal! Not the erotic, sensuous passion of a Gibeah which would crave the body of a single travelling Levite for sexual depravity; but the incredible wickedness of a philosophy that would transform the bodies of countless Jews into fertiliser for cabbages. Gibeah. Gibeah in Europe, this time. The true church, those few people who deliberately set out to serve God, liquidated. Only Niemöller and a pitiful handful like him alive—alive in the death that was a concentration camp.

No wonder God wiped them out. No wonder God ended it. Ended it so totally that many a younger German today can't even imagine how it happened, many can't really believe that it did in fact happen. When Gibeah turns up in human affairs, with no men at all doing what they think is right, when there is no free faith to live at all, then surely the God who is *God* will end it. This is still His world, this is still His purposes being achieved, and never may man or even the devil that is in man hope to make it otherwise. "The light shines on in the dark, and the darkness has never quenched it."

And so I close the Book of Judges. I begin to bundle up my papers and notebook, it is time to think of the new day that is ahead of me. I look up at the window beside me, to see what sort of day it may turn out to be. The sun is already warm and bright as another summer day begins.

For a full year has gone since I began to write about these men and women of three thousand years and more ago. Full cycle, all four seasons, another year in my life. But it certainly hasn't been a year in Palestine with characters out of the long-distant past. No, it has been a year in Sydney with people of my own time and age. Twentieth century, late twentieth century, in fact, with the throb and pulse and sophistication of all that makes up this great metropolis in this vast nation. It has been a year crammed to bursting-point with encounter with my fellow Aussies. Thousands of them, four, perhaps five thousand, in the course of a single year. People in need, people in trouble. Many, many mornings in the operating theatres, at least six days in every week visiting hospitals to do dressings, to watch progress—a very full year indeed.

And yet nothing in this whole over-busy programme has stirred me quite so much as the discovery that this has all been one single experience. The occasional early morning that I have spent with my Bible and with God's case history notes has not in fact turned out to be something different and distant and detached. It is not some quaint schizoid malfunction that operates in a disjointed personality to take him into some escapist studies in an unreal past and which then switches back to a different wavelength to let him resume his place as a modern practising doctor. Far, far from it.

For the simple truth is that I have really been making one single discovery: the discovery of the limitless outgoing of the love of God in His endless concern for the puny struggling of the need of man. And that has always been the same. That is the thing that is utterly constant.

Indeed, it has been the days and days of consultation as a doctor that has given me some real understanding of the occasional pre-dawn encounter with these people out of the past. For their humanity they share alike, modern with old. This man-sized limitation is the thing that is completely common to both. This I have learned.

But it is also the truths which I have seen lived out in the experiences of the Book of Judges that have helped me understand the needs of my patients. Helped me immeasurably. For it is the sweat pouring down the face of Barak as he hears the seeming words of doom: "Up, Barak. Today is the day!" that alone can explain the clinical problem of the man who may well be in my consulting room in just another three hours' time. That searing challenge of the voice of God, the call of Truth, the demand for honesty or courage or any such expression of the essential nature of God who is *God*—that is what really shatters a man. It's not just the challenge to his plans, it's the challenge to his being. Yes, I'll see him today, see him any day.

And the headache that is the presenting symptom in the twenty-year-old lass I will see any day in life at all—that headache is not only the physiological response of meningeal blood-vessels to circulating chemicals. Sure, it is all that. But it is much more than that: it is the heartache due to the emotional challenge in a life that is struggling to find real anchorage, that is in conflict with its own deepest fulfilment and serenity.

Yes, that is really what I have been learning, all this busy
year that is now gone. It is God, God and His ways, God
and His world: that is the real lesson. That is the real discovery.

And now my head is bowed and my heart is quietened as
I put the Book of Judges away. Oh, God, I am praying,
please give me the faith that I have seen so wonderfully
there. The faith that will refuse to separate life into "sacred"
and "secular" compartments, for everything is sacred to
God; the faith that will obey without question when you
say, "Up, John Hercus. Today is the day!"; the faith that
brings every bit of equipment that is in me; the faith that
will spare neither home nor loved one—not even life itself;
the faith that gives free rein to the driving of the Spirit of
God, no matter how hard that driving may seem to be. For
I realise that if this is to be anything, then it is to be everything, for this is how a mere twentieth-century medico may
be re-created into a Son of God ...

And as this wonder begins, in a sad little world where
there is so little light to guide, where so very few know the
King at all, may it be seen that God is indeed *God*, that the
living Christ is in truth alive in His followers. Dear Master,
let me know in my whole life the truth of Your words: "I
am the light of the world. No follower of mine shall wander
in the dark; he shall have the light of life."